THE
CENTURY
SPEAKS

CAMBRIDGESHIRE
voices

One of Kris Neilson's great-uncles (possibly Arthur Player) before his death in the First World War.

THE
CENTURY
SPEAKS

CAMBRIDGESHIRE
voices

Memories of Cambridgeshire people
compiled by Sandra Craft, Katy Elliott and Eva Simmons
alongside the **BBC Radio Cambridgeshire** *series*
The Century Speaks

TEMPUS

First published 1999
Copyright © BBC Radio Cambridgeshire, 1999

Tempus Publishing Limited
The Mill, Brimscombe Port,
Stroud, Gloucestershire, GL5 2QG

ISBN 0 7524 1842 4

Typesetting and origination by
Tempus Publishing Limited
Printed in Great Britain by
Midway Clark Printing, Wiltshire

Cover illustration: A bustling Peterborough street.

A flooded street in Peterborough in the early years of the twentieth century.

CONTENTS

Introduction   6

Acknowledgements   8

1. Where we live   9

2. Identity and community   29

3. Living together   43

4. Crime and the law   59

5. Growing up   65

6. Technology   87

7. Lifestyle   95

8. Living and dying   113

9. Beliefs, fears and the future   121

INTRODUCTION

This book is based on interviews carried out with some 150 people, as part of a Millennium Oral History Project (MOHP) jointly organised by the BBC and the British Library to celebrate the end of the millennium. The Cambridgeshire project was part of a national one to create an archive consisting of interviews with a total of 6,000 people. These will provide a record of the twentieth century, as narrated by those who lived through it. The interviews explored their lives in depth; each one lasted up to two and a half hours, and covered not only their experiences, but their thoughts about these as well as about the century, and indeed about life itself. However, the emphasis was always on the personal narrative, rather than on observations about 'great events'. Subsequently, series of radio programmes were made, together called *The Century Speaks*, to be broadcast on local radio stations throughout the UK. The extracts contained in this book represent just a tiny part of the Cambridgeshire archive.

The finding of interviewees for the project involved appeals on the radio and, directly, to organisations such as local history societies, libraries, and schools, as well as to individuals approached so as to represent, perhaps, a particular category. Many people phoned or wrote in, offering themselves, or suggesting relatives, friends, and acquaintances.

Almost all of the interviews were carried out in the subjects' homes. This made the interviewees more relaxed, and also helped the interviewer to gauge more about each person; vital clues were provided by personal items such as pictures on the walls, ornaments, household furnishings and so on. The interview process was a delight, as contributors told the stories of their lives with humour, fortitude, moving honesty, and above all, fascinating narrative detail. Going into one or two new homes each day was a thrilling experience for the interviewer, like entering into a new world. There was nearly always something unexpected; a story that belied expectations about the person, an unimaginable personal tragedy, or extraordinary achievement made by a supposedly 'ordinary' person, a unique outlook on the world. For me, the project confirmed a long-held view, that although people experience certain things in common, there is no such thing as an ordinary person. Each one is unique and lives life in his or her own way: the life each of us has is perhaps the only one we will ever have, and we live it to the full. By the same token, each life is precious, not only to that individual but to all.

Although the brief for the project was largely similar for all areas, Cambridgeshire posed some specific challenges. The principal one of these was to reflect its diversity as a county, and hence the variety of people living within it. Cambridgeshire is an amalgam of several previously distinct communities, and represents, in a sense, the triumph of the Cambridge area over its neighbours. In the 1930s and 1940s, as the Local Government Boundary Commission deliberated on how to reorganise the region, various parts competed with one another for expansion. The Soke of Peterborough proposed to take over large parts of the Fens (a move dubbed at the time 'Soke's Joke'), Ely attempted to annexe parts of Norfolk, and so on. In the event Cambridgeshire eventually absorbed its neighbours, but old rivalries die hard, and some resentment still remains.

Peterborough in the north-west has an industrial base and, in atmosphere and identity, is effectively part of the East Midlands: until 1965 it was a quasi-autonomous part of Northamptonshire, then it merged briefly with Huntingdon before being absorbed into Cambridgeshire in 1974. Finally, in 1998, it became a unitary authority. This meant that it took responsibility for its own affairs, including education and social services, from Cambridgeshire County Council, although it has remained technically a part of the county of Cambridgeshire. Historically, the people of Peterborough have worked largely in its many factories, especially in engineering, although since the 1980s there has been a decline in manufacturing, resulting in large-scale redundancies.

Wisbech and the north Cambridgeshire Fens are rural in character, sparsely populated, and largely given up to farming. The area is part of the historic county of Cambridgeshire but, despite this, many people who live there feel a greater connection to Norfolk, with which they share a boundary, than with the county town of Cambridge; some have never even been to Cambridge. Traditionally, employment in the area was farming, but with the spread of mechanisation, the way of life associated with farming has all but vanished, and the former farm workers have been dispersed into other industries, retired, or died, and not been replaced.

East Cambridgeshire, with its centre in the cathedral city of Ely, is similar in character to Fenland, although its settlements are less isolated, on the whole, than those of north Cambridgeshire. Together with parts of Fenland, much of the present district formed a separate county, the Isle of Ely, until 1964, when it was merged with Cambridgeshire. Historically, its waterways were important trade routes but, as elsewhere in the country, these diminished in importance with the building of railways and roads. Today there are moves to develop the waterways for leisure and tourism.

Huntingdonshire was a separate county until 1974. Resentment over its absorption into Cambridgeshire still survives and is reflected in the district council's subsequent decision to revive the old county name by changing from 'Huntingdon' to 'Huntingdonshire District Council': an anomaly since there is now no such place as Huntingdonshire, only an administrative entity. The district attempted unsuccessfully to gain the same unitary status accorded to Peterborough in 1998.

Cambridge is dominated by the university but is also historically a small market town without an industrial base. In the second half of the century however it became a focus for burgeoning high technology, and latterly the area has been nicknamed 'Silicon Fen'. South Cambridgeshire consists predominantly of small villages, many of which are filled with commuters to London. In general the district has a more affluent, Home Counties, feel to it than the districts to north and east, and the people have long looked largely to Cambridge and to London for leisure activities as well as jobs. However in recent years the spiralling cost of land in Cambridge has led to the construction of many small business and science parks, providing employment to villagers. Increasingly, such sites are spreading north, east, and west of Cambridge, as well as south.

As a county, Cambridgeshire is one of the fastest growing in Britain (until recently it was the second fastest). The process of expansion dates back at least to the nineteenth century, during which it doubled in size, and by 1971 (before the absorption of Peterborough) it had more than trebled. Historic and social developments have triggered waves of in-migration. The world wars brought evacuees from London, the designation of Peterborough as a New Town led to a huge expansion in the 1970s and '80s – a 30% increase in 1981-91, although individual townships have grown by 100% and more. The high-technology explosion has vastly inflated the populations of Cambridge, South Cambs, and Huntingdonshire. Today, the high property prices have helped to slow down growth in the cities, and East Cambs and Fenland are now the fastest-growing areas – taking in overspill, especially from Cambridge. A new town is being built, Cambourne, west of Cambridge, to house thousands more.

These changes have brought tensions between newcomers and older inhabitants of the county in some areas, especially the Fens, although even here there has been a gradual integration. Many interviewees spoke about their disappearing sense of community. Cambridgeshire's people come from all over the country, and indeed the world, bringing with them diverse customs and attitudes. The population is presently also one of the youngest in the country.

Memories of old times and old ways are still fresh among older people. But attitudes have changed dramatically, together with other social changes. Many people spoke of their own greater affluence, but also of concerns about materialism and rapid technological advances; younger people take these changes for granted. Racism and sexism have diminished in all generations, but especially among the young.

We hope that in this book we have managed to capture some of the compelling interest and variety of Cambridgeshire's voices.

Eva Simmons
September 1999

ACKNOWLEDGEMENTS

Special thanks are due to Chris Jakes and his predecessor, Mike Petty, as well as the staff of the Cambridgeshire Collection, who lent valuable time and expertise as well as photographs for this volume. Peterborough Central Library was also extremely helpful, and lent photographs of the city. Paul Crossley spent hours proof reading and suggesting alterations to the text. Above all, warmest thanks are due to all the people who spent many hours sharing their memories and observations with us, and to those who have trusted us with their precious photographs and memorabilia.

Thanks also to our families and friends for their support and understanding while we undertook this project.

CHAPTER 1
Where we live

A Peterborough back street with the cathedral's spires just poking above the rooftops.

Red Coats

I was born in the village of Cherry Hinton, it was small, with a small school at the end of the village, with a green hut where we used to go for our dinners. It was a farm area, the sheep used to run into the street, and early in the mornings we used to hear the bells…we could see the hunt at the back of the house, men in red coats, and you could see the deer.

Grace Robinson, born 1940

Leaving London

My father was a maintenance man on *The Daily Telegraph*, and I had a friend who also worked in Fleet Street, making paper dress patterns on dummies. I liked the sound of that and so I got a job doing that as well. I worked for *The Chronicle*. I was only about fifteen, and we were on the second floor up, when this air raid started. There were no shelters then, because the raids had only just started. All of a sudden there was a terrific bang, and then a blast and debris came all round us. We went down to the basement, and then all this water came down, because it seemed that the water supply was in a tank in the roof and the bomb or bombs had broken it and set it alight, but the water put it out at the same time. We were smothered in brick dust, and frightened to death. My friend who lived next door worked there too and we walked all the way home to Peckham, scared stiff, and my father said, 'that settles it, you're not going back to the city to be bombed again,

we'll go out in the country to live'. That's how we came to Cambridgeshire.

Meg Tuck, born 1902

Isolated

My mother was a warm countrywoman. We lived in a very isolated situation. The tradesmen came round a few times a week to collect orders and deliver goods. We used to have tickets to the Pantomime in Peterborough and that was a big event, and going to Hunstanton by train was also a big thing. The house was surrounded by fields, in the distance was a silver birch wood, elderberry bushes, it was flooded sometimes, once everywhere flooded.

Terry Huggins, born 1934

Countryside

When we first returned from Indonesia we lived in Cambridge. We looked at houses and saw one or two and preferred the house in Little Thetford. I wanted to move out of town, my wife was less enthusiastic. We had lived in Gwydir Street in Cambridge and parking was impossible, so I decided to move to the countryside.

Bob Young, born 1944

Peterborough

My first impressions of Peterborough were when I was an apprentice. I was among a dozen engineers learning together. When I came to leaving London I recalled my happy times in Peterborough and got a job there. But by then I was married. People were less expert at social conversations, we had lots of dinner parties but they didn't work! You'd drop remarks into a pool of silence they would echo and come back, not like Londoners.

Peterborough then seemed a grim place, but gradually we've built up a close group of friends. We feel totally comfortable in Peterborough now. If I stood on a corner in the centre of Peterborough for five minutes someone would pass by who I know well enough to borrow £10 from! Peterborough has changed enormously. They've rebuilt the city centre, pedestrianized, made country parks, and built the motorway structure around the city. It's a welcoming centre and atmosphere.

We're very happy here and have no desire to leave.

Ken Galloway, born 1936

March

I can recall when the streets of March were almost empty and I could go out with a whipping top or hoop in the middle of the road. Now there's far too much traffic and all the little corner shops have closed down, we used to have the mobile grocer, now it's straight to the supermarket. The railway marshalling yard has gone, now there's the big prison, it brings some strange people to the town. It's not the nice little town it used to be. Now you hear all sorts of accents, Cockney etc. They say March has the biggest migrant population of any town in the county

Market Hill, St Ives, 1900.

because of the cheap property. But the new people expect the same facilities, theatre etc, as if they were still in a big city. But we're hoping for a regeneration project to go through to refurbish the market place, and improve the town hall.

Roy Habbin, born 1925

Sloping Ceiling

We lived in a flat above the ironmonger's shop my father owned in March and had to be very quiet, because if you ran about everyone would hear. I loved to go downstairs, to escape, and weigh nails. I loved to go out on the delivery van, delivering paraffin and fireplaces. From age five onwards my father was in the shop all the time, and my mother was in the flat looking after us. We were in the roof space, I slept in a room with a sloping ceiling, which was exciting, my window overlooked the police station and the courtroom, there were court sessions on Tuesdays, and there was always a lot going on, the police garages were behind.

Diana Philipott, born 1951

My Cat

My father decided he wanted to leave the city and be out in the open, to escape the bombing in London, and for his health. We saw a smallholding advertised in Chatteris, so we moved there to run a poultry farm. I remember arriving, the long walk to the station from the house. I had a cat which I loved and played with, I preferred him to dolls. This cat was in a basket and I lugged him on foot, all the way from the station. I had always fed him on cat's meat, and in Clapham the cat meat man used to come round with his basket and push it through the letter-box, and the cat would sit underneath waiting for it to fall through. But in Chatteris I didn't know what to feed him on, because there wasn't much meat about, so he got fed up, went out and caught rabbits and brought them home to eat! After a time, my father got some rabbits and kept them for food so we had them to eat, but unfortunately the cat killed some of the young rabbits, and one day my father got so angry, he killed the cat. I was heartbroken.

Meg Tuck, born 1902

Refugees

My family are Polish, not Jewish but Catholic, and my mother came from Poland. After the Nazis occupied Poland, my mother kept running away, and she was taken to Auschwitz. But she escaped from there too and survived the war. She managed to get to Italy, and was helped by British soldiers. She met my father in Italy, and came to England. I was born here, one of six children. We lived in huts, in refugee camps in Essex and in Suffolk, with other Polish refugees. They were nice places, we had our own church, a cinema; we did our traditional dances in traditional costumes. It was a happy environment, we congregated in the

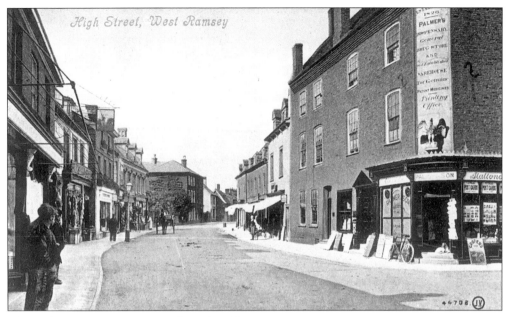

The High Street, West Ramsey, in the early 1900s.

church and at the shops. Later the refugees were housed in new towns, we were sent to Harlow. I always spoke to my mother in Polish, I didn't speak English until I was five, and I still think in both Polish and English. Five years ago I went to Poland and met my Polish relatives. They're proud of having a relative in England.

Anna Wiseman, born 1949

Black Lead

Our street lights were gas mantles with fine mesh, even in the home we had gas mantles. We had electricity in the end, but then my mother used to cook on an old range, a black lead thing and she used to blacklead it and then rub it up with velvet to make it shine extra nice, and all the brass fender with all the long tools. Everything my

mother had that was brass, even the pipes that went up, the water pipes, shone and the window knobs, my mother was a very house-proud person, she loved her home, a lot of people did. We had a small garden at the front with rose bushes and another at the back with rose bushes, then another piece of land further on where you grew your vegetables, then another piece behind that.

Grace Robinson, born 1940

Contrasts

I remember coming back to the Fens as an adult, the contrast: when I lived there as a child, you could leave your back door open, but when I returned we kept getting things stolen, until a woman I knew who styled herself as a witch let it be known that she would put a spell on whoever had stolen my crockery, and I got it back!

Billie Bridgement, born 1935

Wash-Day in Soham

Monday was wash day, and the neighbours had a competition to see who could get their washing out first. I'm sure one woman cheated and got hers done on a Sunday, because she was always first! The washing took most of the day: we had no gas or electric, only paraffin and coal – and logs. You had to light a fire in the copper, you put a log of wood under the copper, it stuck out into the room and you had to push it further under as it burned. You had a blue bag to keep the clothes white, and you had to scrub the clothes using a brush and a scrubbing board. Then it all had to be put through a big mangle. The common land where the women hung out their washing became farm-land – it was taken over in the war. The Government had powers to take over agricultural land. Later it belonged to a private farmer, but no-one ever complained that the common land was lost!

John Martin, born 1926

Gypsy Camp Fire

I've lived on my gypsy caravan site at Oxney Road, on the outskirts of Peterborough, for twenty-five years. I'm from Kingston upon Hull. I came to this site because I heard about a trailer for sale. I came here to get away from the harassment you get when you travel, for a peaceful life. But I miss the travelling way of life. You could stop anywhere

The Holywell Ferry, near St Ives, 1900.

A Peterborough Street with a tram and a horse-drawn carriage.

along the road and start up a fire, within moments other gypsies would join you and you'd sit round the fire together, you might not have seen any other gypsies at all on your way, but within moments they'd be there. We're part of a larger community. My home is where my trailer is, I still don't feel like I belong in Peterborough, even though I've been here so long and work for the city council. I'm a gypsy, and I belong with other gypsies. You give up a lot when you choose to settle.

Peter Mercer, born 1935

Friendly

I remember being pushed round St Ives in a pram and being taken to see the manager of the shoe shop where my mother had worked. It was a small market town, but seemed large, and fascinating. Then it had 4,000 people, by the time I left it had grown beyond recognition. But it had more facilities then: A railway station, cinema, banks, and shops. Now a lot has gone. Today you leave and go to another town to shop, then you didn't travel as far, and you

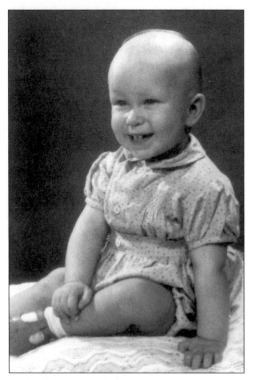

Richard Carter as a baby.

expected everything to be on your doorstep.

Richard Carter, born 1955

Country Folk

I have been involved with agriculture all my life. My first home was at a farm in Holme Fen, near Peterborough and Warboys. It was two miles from the main road. The house was a wooden structure with feather boards outside and tongue and groove inside. It had no electricity and no water. Water came down from the roof and my mother collected it and put it in stone in the pantry. The river was close to the house, and we used river water for washing.

Terry Huggins, born 1934

Cathedral Square, Peterborough.

Dora Ellis (soon to be Dora Tack) shortly after she met Frank Tack, 1941. From left to right: Frank Tack, Dora Ellis, Sylvia Jenkins, Arthur Sibley.

Mother and Father

I have lived in Huntingdon since 1940. I was born in London, but left during the blitz. My mother came from Tunbridge Wells, and my father came from Godmanchester. They met when my mother was in service, he was a new hall boy and she told him off for wheeling his bike across the floor. They courted by postcards when my father was in India, he got home in 1919 and he joined the police in 1920.

Dora Tack, born 1921

Cosmopolitan

I moved to my present house twenty-six years ago when I was teaching at UC College in London and wanted to be able to commute, to use King's Cross or St Pancras. I couldn't afford a house any nearer London, so I chose Huntingdon. I still commute to London sometimes by train, and sometimes by motorbike. I have also lived in Denmark. My grandparents were Jewish refugees who came over from Russia after a pogrom. My parents and their brothers and sisters were born here. My parents were born in 1909 and 1911 and they married in 1944. It was my mother's second marriage and I was born in 1948; I have a half-brother, who is older, from my mother's first marriage.

Michael Black, born 1948

Dens and Ditches

I grew up in Castle Camps, as a child I played in dens and ditches. I had three younger brothers, triplets, two identical and the other not. I felt privileged being older, and the only girl. I felt motherly towards them.

Maria Daines, born 1963

Cosy

When I was a child, because I lived in a flat I didn't have freedom to go out into a garden. We were on a main road and mother was worried. My own children have a garden to play in. It's in a relatively safe area to ride a bike, so their life is probably nicer, they're in a safer environment, but I enjoyed our flat because it was cosy and my father was always downstairs if I needed to talk to him. You always had to go through the shop to go anywhere. I have always been close to my parents and grandparents, I could take my doll's pram and go round to my grandmother, we watched *Emergency Ward 10* on television, and listened to the radio. Then at Christmas time we'd always play games or cards, it was nice, you communicated with each other.

Diana Philipott, born 1951

Changing Roles

My mother's family comes from Manchester, my dad's from Leicester, they came to Isleham because of work. My mother has only worked for a few years. Some years ago dad became unemployed so she had to start working to help get an income, and since then she's not stopped. When she was at home she had to look after the children, but now we're all at school, there's nothing for her to do. When my father

Inside Johnson's, March, in the 1950s.

18

Flooded fields, St Ives. St Ives has a tendency to succumb to flooding.

was made redundant we got no pocket money, no holidays, and he stayed at home to look after us.

Andrew Dunkley, born 1985

Being Crowned

I recall seeing the Coronation of George V and Mary, and I thought 'fancy them being crowned in a little place like Hemingford', but it was only the celebrations that were happening in the village!

Jack Harrison, born 1907

Stories

I used to live out in the Fens, my grandparents lived in the house I grew up in and they were smallholders. They told me stories of the Italians and the Germans who were around, and they used things the POW's had made, such as cigarette lighters and ornaments.

Peter Brown, born 1935

Happy Times

Born and bred in Cambridge, my first home was in Hale Street near the Rex Cinema. Life was unsophisticated then, we had an outdoor loo. My father turned it into an indoor loo and a nice bathroom.

It was our own home and it was so happy, my father and mother were good, easy-going, and things were good, not like now. There were no class distinctions, no worries about race. Everybody was happy together. Our neighbours were working class.

The atmosphere of Cambridge has changed immensely with its expansion, in the old days you had to have a financial background to go to the university. That's changed and I'm glad of it, in that sense things have changed for the better. But people in the city are conservative, in the north people are much friendlier.

Peter Hoskison, born 1933

Afterthought

I had three older brothers and was spoilt, I was an 'afterthought', the youngest and the only girl in the family. I was petted, and taken everywhere. We had a Tate and Lyle sugar box with wheels and they carted me around everywhere.

Meg Tuck, born 1902

Pleasant World

I was born at Kneesworth, into a pleasant world, despite the war. I remember ration books, police warning 'Lights out, zeppelins about'. Both my parents were at home, and life was quiet and comfortable, I was not aware of war.

A Bassingbourn Sunday school outing to Royston Heath in 1923, which included Geoffrey Allgood.

20

A young Dorothy Grubb at a wedding in December 1912.

I grew my own vegetables. It was cold in the cottage, and it had a dirt floor. Now I have a gas fire which looks like a coal fire.

People grew their own food and kept animals. There were some queues at the Labour Exchange in Letchworth, but it was a small town, so the queues weren't that long, but there were some empty factories. I remember reading about the Jarrow March in the papers, but my friends and I had jobs. I knew some people out of work but they didn't seem to worry too much.

Geoffrey Allgood, born 1913

Bus Service

When I first came to Cambridgeshire I lived in the village of Yelling; the bus services were so poor you could only get into Huntingdon once a week, so I applied for housing in St Neots and got my present flat.

Dorothy Grubb, born 1908

Loss of Identity

I remember when Huntingdonshire became part of Cambridgeshire, St Neots had been a town with its own identity, its own town and district council, its own amenities, a little council depot with its own characters that worked for the town council. You knew the people, the same ones. In Huntingdonshire, St Neots was like the jewel in the crown; when Huntingdonshire got absorbed into

Anniversary celebrations of the birth of Oliver Cromwell, Huntingdon, April 1999.

Cambridgeshire, St Neots lost its importance and became just like any other small place.

Paul Anger, born 1962

Escape the Crowds

Little Thetford was once a very small village with four or five farms, most people worked on the farms. The main industry was coprolite. There was a close community when I arrived. World War Two didn't take quite as many people from the village as World War One. Everybody grew vegetables, everything was there. You went into the garden and dug up what you needed. Beer was brewed. It changed from being a very old community to being quite a young community in the 1950s. Some people were very opposed to the expansion. A lot of people who came to the village to escape the crowds now find they're back where they came from, because they're surrounded by houses.

The school is no longer a village school, more an area school, so now there's a traffic problem. The A10 isn't a dual carriageway and it's busy. My grandfather would ride along it and you wouldn't see a car.

In all villages you get ups and downs but there are still enough people who've lived in the village for many years, but the balance is changing. For some people there is a 'them and us' feeling; just as there's sexism and racism, there's 'new villagerism'.

Tony Badcock, born 1936

Property

I was born in St Neots, and now I live in Mepal. I remember the first house I lived in, in St Neots. It was a small two-up, two-down workman's cottage.

Our house was bought by the council under a compulsory purchase order. They wanted to knock the houses down and build a car park. It never happened, they found they couldn't buy the other side of the road. But they would only pay my parents the knock down value of the property, so they couldn't afford to buy anywhere else and this was really shameful to them that, having had their own property, they then had to go back into rented accommodation.

Judy Fox, born 1955

Many Changes

When I was a child we had no bathroom, we used a tin bath. Going to the toilet meant a trek across the yard and the horror of having to go downstairs in the dark. Economically we were all roughly the same, the area where I lived has been knocked down, and our street renamed. There was an abattoir nearby. It was a great place to live.

We used to race on soapboxes up and down the road. That's no longer possible. A lot of people came from the London area, also servicemen and their families. Many moved away, including my friends. St Ives Town Council went for expansion through private housing. So they never experienced the problems of St Neots and Huntingdon, where the big council estates were built. My parents rented our home and paid the same rent for many years. Then we moved to a wonderful new house with all mod cons in 1966. It was part of the huge change St Ives went through. A lot of the allotments have gone, people don't want to grow vegetables any more when they can go down to the supermarket and buy them ready-washed. I remember we used to collect blackberries and my mother would bottle and freeze them and other fruit.

Richard Carter, born 1955

Nice to be Here

I was born in Newbury, Berkshire and came to Cambridge aged eighteen months. I now live in more or less the

Richard Carter aged eight or nine with his cousin Margaret and brother Christopher.

The old Rex Cinema, Cambridge, 1971.

same area where I grew up near Mill Road, the Romsey area. My grandfather worked on the railways and houses were built for people who worked on the railways, it's nice to still be in the area.

Now I'm less than ten minutes walk from where I grew up, things are still very familiar, some things have changed, but there are still lots of small shops, but fewer butchers and no fishmongers. Many of the general small shops have been replaced with specialist ones.

Lynne Hester, born 1960

Idyllic

I live in Market Deeping, but come from Apethorpe in Northants. My life has spanned three counties, but I feel more of a Cambridgeshire person than anything else. We moved to a tied cottage, I don't remember much, probably because I needed glasses, and then when I was eight and got glasses a whole world opened up. I didn't learn to read until I was seven. My teacher hated me and she told my parents that I was hateful, and the worst child she'd met in her teaching career. She wasn't interested in my education. I was a '60s child and spoilt, I expected things my own way. It wasn't until the 'Nit Lady' came and said, 'this child can't see'.

The new house was in a fabulous area. There was a river at the bottom of the garden. The environment was safe, I could pick mushrooms in the field, cycle on my bike, it had a *Cider with Rosie* feel to it, idyllic, a horse-chestnut tree. We'd paddle in the brook, in the summer trout would jump up from the brook onto the grass. Lads from the village would swim in the field when it flooded into the road and cars couldn't get through.

Linda Hill, born 1961

Bungalow

After I was married, we had a bungalow, although we had to completely gut it. We gradually built it up, we added rooms. It was special to us because we put so much time and effort into it. When our second child was born there wasn't enough room, so we bought the current house, but it'll never be like the bungalow was, because we put so much work into it and built it up together.

Diana Philipott, born 1951

Starting Out

I'm originally from Grimsby, but came to Peterborough when I was sixteen. I had left school at fifteen, and went to a pre-apprenticeship course in Grimsby. A friend was going to Peterborough so I went too and got work with Perkins Engines. I'm still working there. I started out as an apprentice, most factories take very few now, but Perkins still takes quite a few, and I train them.

Brian Pearce, born 1949

Gypsy Caravan Site

I have lived all my life on the Oxney Road gypsy caravan site. It's a good site; a close community. But it has its bad side, people who commit crimes. I remember many people who have died or moved on, and fruit picking when I was a child. There was more spirit then; it was better when I was young, because there were more young people, now many have moved away. You don't leave your travelling way of life though. What are different are the traditions and culture of gypsies.

Charmayne Mercer, born 1978

Mill Road, Cambridge, 1900.

Wisbech Market Place, 1931.

Soham

Until now I've lived in Soham. My earliest home was in the north end of Soham, near the Common Land. The smallholders would graze their animals there. The house had a scullery and a dairy. My mother died eleven days after I was born and an elder sister brought me up. She was nineteen when I was born.

John Martin, born 1926

Armistice

I was born in Fordham, but have been living in Ely for fourteen years. My father was a land worker, he went into the Army and worked for Lord Derby who was the War Minister. He was in the Signalling Service, Suffolk Regiment. He was taken prisoner in Belgium, he came back after the Armistice. My younger brother was born six or seven days after the Armistice, my father arrived home a few days later, but my mother died in childbirth just before he got back. So he had to cope with a dead wife and seven children.

Harry Bye, born 1917

Adopted

From Hitchin I was adopted at birth and moved to High Wycombe. My parents were evacuated because their earlier house was bombed. We moved when I was three or four to the American Hospital at Wimpole Hall. It was a lively, fun place.

I was illegitimate. I have no knowledge of my parents.

Bill Wicksteed, born 1945

A Better Place

I grew up in London but came to live in Cambridge in the 1920s. At first we lived in Burrells Walk. It had no kitchen, no bathroom, no sink; I had to carry water in pails. Other Londoners were living there, and I made friends

John Martin in 1948.

Harry Bye, aged two, and his father in 1919. This picture was taken at Sheffards Studios in Soham just before his father was demobbed.

27

Raymond Law with his father, 1940s.

with them. I got a job in a college as a
bed-maker, but had problems with my
feet and needed hospital treatment. We
moved to Malcolm Street and were able
to rent rooms to students. It was a much
better place to live.

Alice Humm, born 1893

CHAPTER 2
Identity and community

Histon, in the 1950s.

Gypsies

The gypsies used to come and set up in the end of the spinney, we used to go and make friends with them, they were never any fear to us, they used to come round selling the pegs that they made, wooden ones with a metal clip at the top. Then they'd knock on your door to see if you wanted to buy a lace. In the late '40s, early '50s you had the people coming round with turbans on their heads and suitcases; Indians and other Asians, ethnic people we had never seen before, selling stuff at your door: lace, silk, cotton, handkerchiefs, 'you buy Missy, you buy'! It was quite funny, it was a friendly neighbourhood. The Indians must have come up from London, we didn't even know London existed, we'd never been on a train, you never thought of how people got there, because cars were few and far between.

Grace Robinson, born 1940

Country Person

I was a rebel, and once I had a black boyfriend. He was quite big and completely bald, my parents and the village were quite shocked. There are still quite strong pockets of racism, and lack of understanding of other cultures and creeds, particularly in this area where we lack the diversity of industrial cities. It's quite a shock still to people, whereas I find it difficult that people of a different colour should be treated differently, it doesn't cross my mind.

Linda Hill, born 1961

Frowned Upon

My background is Anglo-Indian, my mother was English, and father was Portuguese, mixed with Indian and African. He was the only black man allowed in my mother's family's house. There was a stigma in whites marrying Indians, it wasn't illegal, but frowned upon, and remarked upon. People say the Anglo-Indian life was a parody of English life, but it was the only way we knew. I was brought up on Enid Blyton stories from England. I'm the type of person who sits on the fence, and looks over to both sides, and laughs at both sides. I am neither English nor Indian, but something distinct.

Ernest Ignatius, born 1944

A Colourful Neighbourhood

Everybody in Soham knew each other, and all our neighbours had names of colours – Mrs Brown, Mrs White, Mrs Green etc. Once somebody came looking for a Mrs Black, but we told him he had the wrong colour!

John Martin, born 1926

Home Country

We moved to Little Thetford so the children could go to the King's School in Ely, and also for the sake of the village environment; before that they'd lived in Jakarta, Indonesia. We returned to England to give our children a secondary education in the home country.

Bob Young, born 1944

Ernie Ignatius and his band in India.

Different

I'm from an Asian background and my husband is Afro-Caribbean. There are no other Asians around, in the school there are a lot of blonde-headed children, and not many from mixed backgrounds. There aren't big problems, but my children notice they're different. I was born in Bombay.

Louella Prince, born 1961

Backward

My father died and I've often wondered why I and my mother never went back to London, but we didn't. I still think of myself as a Londoner – I don't speak like a country person, do I? I think I'm a bit sharper than local people. I felt that when I arrived, the children and everyone seemed so backward. They had to walk long journeys to school, about three miles there and back. The poor transport situation struck me, because I had been used to horse buses and the beginning of motor buses in London, and there was no transport in Chatteris, that's why they didn't get milk, not until the Mepal Milk Delivery Service started up. But then they knew other things which I didn't know: about crops, for example, wheat, barley, corn, it was marvellous to me to see the corn ripe and the rye ripe in the fields. I knew

31

milk came from a cow but I didn't know where or how. We came to love it, everything was so much cleaner and brighter, the flowers all seemed bigger.

Meg Tuck, born 1902

Stretham

I'm still living in the village where I grew up (Stretham), but sometimes I feel a stranger in my own community. I can't say whether I still feel part of the village. I know its history, I'm on the parish council and I've been a governor of the village school and a charity trustee, but I can't say I know the village. I can give a talk in a village and it seems to have a great community spirit, but I can go back five years later and the spirit has changed, the village has changed. In many places, such as the village of Reach, when someone arrived, he was the only newcomer, now thirty years later he's the only one left of the old-timers. It's happening everywhere. I don't now know a lot of people, there're coming in all the time.

Mike Petty, born 1946

Racism

My biological parents were Jamaican. I experience racism everyday, but now it's subtler, less obvious than it used to be, so it's more difficult to confront. Cambridge is multi-cultural for a small city. Everyone else in my family is white,

Mill Road, Cambridge in 1978.

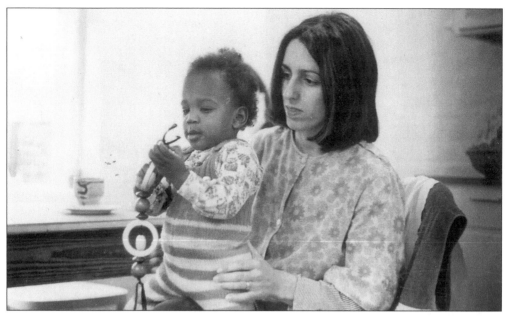

Dominique Elliott with her mother, Jean, in 1974.

we always have to explain the family history, and that I'm adopted.

Dominique Elliott, born 1973

Where The Work Is

Gypsies travel to where the work is. In Wisbech we picked strawberries, we worked from 7 a.m. to 4 p.m. and then did our own work and went to sleep at 10 p.m. in the summer.

Louise Loveridge, born 1914

A German POW

My father came from Czechoslovakia, and my mother from Germany. My father fought in the German Army in the Second World War. It's strange, I could so easily have been brought up somewhere else. My father was from peasant surroundings, he was a Sudeten Deutscher, a German-speaking Czech, and his hometown was just a few kilometres across the border from Germany. He was in Austria serving an apprenticeship when the Germans and the Austrians got back together in the Anschluss, and he chose to join the forces in 1938. He had been a civilian, skiing in the Alps, and he joined the German mountain troops. He served in Salzburg; he was also in Stalingrad, one of the few to survive that. One of the first things to impact on me when I was in my early teens was a visit to Duxford airfield in Cambridgeshire, seeing an aeroplane, an old German JU52: to me it wasn't a bomber or fighter or anything, but my father patted it on the side and said, 'best plane in the world, it flew me out of Stalingrad'. That was the worst image of what could happen in war – total annihilation of both sides with no winner. My father was also in Yugoslavia, father fought with the Croatians and Germans against Tito and the Partisans. He finished his war in Italy, Montecasino, and surrendered in 1945 to the British. He was interned in Cheshire, also in Graveley and at Great Gransden in Cambridgeshire. There were a lot of POW camps in that area, in the Gransdens. After the war, my father didn't go back to Czechoslovakia, because the Russians had occupied it by then, he couldn't go back, and he didn't know what had happened to his family, so he stayed in Britain. A farmer whom he'd worked for as a prisoner of war offered him a job and he took it. He met my mother in Cheshire, she was from Hanover in Germany and, at that time, she was working for the Red Cross. They married and moved down to St Neots, and I was born there.

Paul Anger, born 1962

Equality

For me gender is most important because my father used to make girls do the washing up while the boys watched football. The way my father behaved belittled my mother; I didn't want to be like my mother, although now I'm amazed how she coped with five children. I'm a better person because of my experiences, but I wouldn't want my children to cope with what I did, it is important to have equality at home. A relationship with equality is more likely to last.

Melissa Baxter, born 1976

Raymond Law's parents, 1933.

Kris Neilson, July 1999.

Comfortable

I feel different because I'm adopted and I'm black, my sisters aren't adopted. I'm not different in a negative way. I don't know where I belong, this is often an issue for mixed race adoptions, culturally where do you belong? I feel comfortable in a number of places, and around different people, but I wouldn't like to live in the Fens, it's the middle of nowhere.

Dominique Elliott, born 1973

First Impressions

We came to Cambridge to live. I recall my first impression of Cambridge; quiet, but the birds were noisy. I still think of myself as a 'towny' though now I wouldn't leave Sutton.

Many of my neighbours are from London, some came from Norfolk, and all are from somewhere else. I don't know any locals, one of my neighbours says we're not in each others' pockets, we keep ourselves to ourselves, but if there were an emergency they'd be there.

Raymond Law, born 1938

Danish

My name is Neilson, my grandfather was a Danish sailor who was washed up in England, and he married an English girl, my grandmother. I married an Englishman, but my Danish heritage is important to me.

Kris Neilson, born 1949

The Workforce Changed

I started at Pye in 1956-57 and worked there, right up until 1990. The size of the workforce changed over that time, also the attitude – I mean it was basically women, and men did test work, that was before equality came in, and also it was only the men that could have the apprenticeships. So it was basically women did the cable forming, the menial jobs. Plus the fact that it seemed the women's hands were more supple than men's, they were smaller hands to get into corners. Then as time went on, the women were doing more, at first the men were doing the test work, but in later years the women were doing the test repairs, women were getting into the drawing sides of it, designing and everything, they were equal. Women were made in charge of

Diana Philpott, pre-motherhood, 1976.

sections and then boys started coming on the line, and then in later years you started getting the ethnic people coming in, and the Germans, Austrians, whatever were coming in there that came to live in this country, so you got a wide variety of people.

Grace Robinson, born 1940

Speaking German

At home my parents spoke German; it was difficult for me, going to school, speaking English, then going home to German, I pronounced some consonants in the German way. My mother found English very hard, also my father until late in his life. I'm fluent in German, I picked it up: When I was ten/eleven years old we used to go back to Germany often, so I had to pick up the language in order to survive. At school I wanted to do German. I had done French badly, and the teacher told me I would never learn German, but I replied to him in German – he was quite surprised!

Paul Anger, born 1962

Who's Doing What

Where I live now I know a lot of people from the days when I used to collect debts for a company, it was very difficult. I was followed once and threatened. We have our own community council on the estate, to run the community's affairs, we decide on fund-raising projects. This area, having had a bad name, now has a community spirit. Some areas have less of that. A year ago hypodermic needles were found in the toddlers' area of the recreation ground, someone found out who it was and shopped them to the police.

People know who's doing what, there's a network of people supplying drugs. I know who they are but don't let on; I don't know what they deal in. It was the people that did know who actually shopped them. We don't want drugs in the area and we now have our community policeman back and the attitudes to the police have changed a lot. It's not such a violent estate as it used to be.

Sandra Wells, born 1955

The Future

I don't feel a particular regional identity, not like someone I know who's Welsh. I'm not big on local history like my mother, I tend to look to the future rather than to the past, I don't dwell on the past.

Gavin Philpott, born 1980

Acceptance

If I married out it would be easier to be accepted by the non-gypsy community, than for a non-gypsy to be accepted by the gypsies. They would never be trusted; you'd be welcomed, but not accepted. It is changing but still exclusive. Occasionally you do get mixed marriages. You never leave your community properly; it would be hard to be without the community's support.

Gavin Philpott (Diana's son) on holiday in Scotland, 1999.

You can be talking to someone outside the community who is very friendly, then you tell them you're from the caravan site and they turn their backs, but others are interested, you strike up a conversation in a shop, doctor's surgery, wherever. I have applied for jobs and found hostility from the prospective employers, mostly jobs in the food industry. Many people are racist and prejudiced, they lack understanding and fear the unknown.

Charmayne Mercer, born 1978

Ethel Law and foster son, Jason, in the backyard of their Willburton house, 1971.

Out

I'm gay and could never be interested in women, heterosexual images in society don't bother me but I find it very difficult to get hold of gay videos. Attitudes locally vary, in Peterborough there's a lot of homophobic bullying and you can't be 'out', but in Cambridge you can be. You could hold hands there and you wouldn't get shouted at, in Peterborough you would be because they're undereducated and fear something that's different.

Being gay transcends classes, in a gay club you forget class. I go to gay clubs and gay evenings. I work for Tesco stores; I work nights only, unloading goods. I prefer nights, I don't need sleep, you get fewer hassles at night. I get on with my mates. At a previous job in Warboys I had a lot of hassle, so I left. Men and women can be equally abusive. In my home sex was and is a taboo subject, all I learned was at school and that was exclusively heterosexual sex. I had formal sex education at school, but I didn't relate to any of it.

Edward Venni, born 1974

Anti-German

There's a lot of anti-German feeling, jingoism, in Britain: My father took it to the grave with him and would say he was better off under the Nazis than in Britain. But personally, I haven't found the jingoism hard. In the end, I can produce my passport which says I'm British – I was born here and this is my mother country: I'm as English and British as the next person, only my roots are a little bit deeper and broader than other people born in St Neots and bred in St Neots. The bottom line is I was born and brought up in Britain and have served in Her Majesty's Armed Forces: I was in the Army and served in the Falklands, and in Northern Ireland. That shows my loyalty. But Germany is part of my roots – it's somewhere else to go, where I could settle down quite happily. During a European Championships match when Britain and Germany played against each other, I wanted England to win – and then, Germany! Actually, I felt that whoever won, I couldn't lose!

Paul Anger, Born 1962

Humour

Fenland people are more prepared to work at things than other people, my wife once threatened to leave me so I offered to help her pack and we ended up laughing. It helps to be mad to live in the Fens and to have a sense of humour. They're all comedians round here, they're wonderful people, the humour comes from way back, walking in the mud, making your own entertainment.

Brian Abblitt, born 1948

Terrible Place

When I lived in Cambridge years ago the undergraduates lived all around in absolute squalor, colleges took no notice. Cambridge is a terrible place now, no shops, all language schools, and no service. Our old house, when I sold it, was turned into a lodging house and went into decay.

Phillis Hounsell Parker, born 1917

Youth Worker

Now that I'm a youth worker it helps me to feel I belong here in Cambridge. I meet people on the streets and that too makes me feel more at home. To me community is affected by people I work with: Poverty-stricken families, it's harder for them, they have riches rubbed in their faces. I talk to groups, and try to keep them occupied. I

Harry Bye's work mates undertake back-breaking work at Burnt Fen.

39

give them something to join in, they play, incorporate their own ideas. They sometimes get into trouble and tell me about it, one girl 'disclosed' her problems and I was fighting back the tears, but that's not good, because they need to focus on themselves, not me.

Melissa Baxter, born 1976

Anti-Semitic

I'm not married to a Jew, so my children are only half-Jewish. I believe there's a lot of latent anti-Semitism in Britain, it's just that English people are not so physically expressive in the way they show it, it's more subtle. In 1979-80 my daughter was badly beaten up at her primary school in Cambridge. For years nobody had done anything to hurt her, and then one day a well-meaning teacher asked her to get up and tell the other children about the Jewish Passover Festival, because it was that time of year. Afterwards she was attacked, and as they were hitting her, the children kept calling her an 'F-ing Jew'. But the headmistress kept denying that there was anti-Semitism in the school and refused to deal with it. We took her out of there and moved her to another school, Queen Edith's, where there was no anti-Semitism at all. I only found out last week that the same treatment had gone on in the secondary school in Cambridge. It must have come from the parents, those attitudes, where else could the children have got them from? Until then, I had brought the girls up without religion, but after that I decided they must have a Jewish education, and I got involved with the Jewish Community in Cambridge.

Etel Shepherd, born 1934

Bridge Street, St Ives, 1914.

40

Bad Reputation

Where I live in my small housing estate in Cambridge is a community; people are very kind and concerned. There are a great variety of people, all races and nationalities, if you have a problem, you can knock on a door and someone will help. The neighbourhood has had a bad reputation for drug taking and crime, but they're mostly really lovely people.

Sally Scott, born 1965

Unfriendly

My parents owned their home eventually, but the house was sold when they died. My husband and I could never afford to own a house; we lived by farming, smallholding, and made very little money, especially through the winter months.

Then it was a community, but now if you need people to help, you can't find it. Where my daughter lives at Hemingford is an unfriendly community.

Lillian Melton, born 1932

A Japanese Voice

The worst aspect of being a prisoner of war was hearing a Japanese voice, we really detested it. Many years later, after I returned to my college in Cambridge, I was told that a Japanese conference was coming there. I asked to be excused, saying that I couldn't bear to hear the voices, but then I heard the voices of an advance party, and suddenly, on an impulse, I went outside and talked to them in Japanese, they were astonished. I had looked down the list of people attending the conference, and one of the names was the same as the villain who was in charge of the death camp. I spoke to this man, but he assured me that his father was a jeweller, and had never been a military officer! Later I was pleased that I didn't take a month off when the Japanese conference group came, because they were the most charming people, completely different from the brutal officers that I remembered. I'd seen the two sides then, and I felt that I'd resolved something. I even corresponded with some of them when they went back to Japan. Once, when I was decorating salmon for their meals, they took photographs of me (and it!) and sent them to me.

Stanley Chown, born 1911

Sexism

During the war I worked in a tool room with four women. Some men were very resentful of them, especially the foreman, he was a stick-in-the-mud. I began to campaign that we were doing exactly the same job as the men and getting two-thirds of the wages. Some of the women who came down from Scotland to work couldn't afford to pay for their accommodation and couldn't survive on the money they were getting. We had a campaign, it involved a strike, even though this was illegal; muted, no publicity as there would be today. Women were still in a subsidiary role,

Joan Mulgrew and her husband on their wedding day, 1 January 1952.

wife and homemaker. The war made some irreversible changes, though efforts were made to reverse them, but from then women started to progress slowly.

Joan Mulgrew, born 1920

CHAPTER 3

Living together

The Romsey town end of Mill Road, in Cambridge, with the railway bridge in the background.

Traced After Fourteen Years

Father didn't know where my mother was – he had tried to find her once, and brought her back, but she went off again – you could trace them through their ration books then, or their insurance number – but the second time she went, near my birthday, she never took a ration book with her, so you couldn't trace her, they gave up then. I found her by luck, via an aunt. My mother was always for dogs and always called her dogs Patsy. There was a bit in the paper about this Irish wolfhound-cross that was an alcoholic dog in London. It used to go to the Anchor pub, and it was in the papers, and my aunt picked it out and showed me it, and it had got Mary Shannon which was my mother, and she called the dog Patsy, and that's how I traced her, after fourteen years. So I would be twenty-six, I'd got my son then. I just got on the train and went to London, knocked on this door, and found her. I looked through this window, to the flat above, and she recognised me, after fourteen years. And I got her in touch with all the family then, her mother and her aunts. She broke down and cried, and then we got on with life.

We weren't a family that could put our arms round each other and come and say 'I love you', it wasn't ever done.

Grace Robinson, born 1940

Instant Love

My mother never talked to me about sex or anything, she just always wanted me to marry someone rich, and that was it! My husband works with computers, adapting them, but we don't have a lot of money. Having my son was the best day of my life; it was such a mystery, to give birth to another human being even after over fifty hours of labour. I recall putting him on my tummy; it was amazing and instant love.

Lynne Hester, born 1960

Marriage

My husband and I married quite soon after we met. Everyone thought I was pregnant, but I wasn't and still have no children after fifteen years. We married in a Register Office. It was unbelievable. During the ceremony I felt so emotional I started to cry, at which Steve put his hand out and held my hand, at which point everybody started to cry. There were about sixty people, all in tears! It was August 27th 1983 and baking hot, so hot the confetti stained my dress. We had our reception at the Falcon, Fotheringay, where Mary Queen of Scots met her doom! I was so nervous I couldn't eat anything at the reception! It was lovely and we went off to Paris for our honeymoon. It was really romantic.

Linda Hill, born 1961

Remarkable Experience

I was born in London, but have been in Cambridge for nearly thirty years. I had a remarkable experience this morning. For going on twenty-five years I had lost contact with my three children. This morning I found a letter from the

Salvation Army, about making contact with my daughter. I had a bitter divorce from my ex-wife. For many years I wrote to my children but my ex didn't pass the letters on. Meanwhile my daughter has had many arguments with her mother and realises I may not be entirely to blame. When I met Jean I was very young, seventeen. We were both too young. We lived in various naval depots, but never settled. We had three children very quickly and began to have arguments. Then I started to meet other women and it all blew up.

Len Baynes, born 1937

Mistake

After we married, he kept me short of money all the time. We should never have married, looking back; I married him to get away from home. All the parents thought we were making a mistake. I remember him getting quite nasty when I was expecting our daughter Jayne. He was going out with someone else and my emotions were all up the shoot. He was very lazy, and would always stay late in bed. One Saturday he swore at me and I threw a cup and saucer at him, then another, he thought I had to bow down to him all the time, it was very turbulent the whole time.

Sandra Wells, born 1955

Corresponding

I was a fellow of Clare College and I went on a Bavarian skiing holiday and met my wife. Later I read her diary, and she wrote

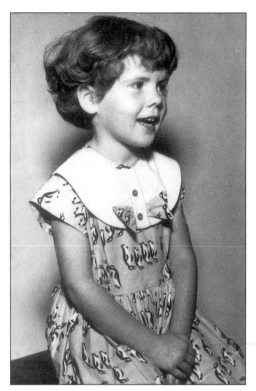

Sandra Wells, aged four.

'I'm madly in love with Brian Reddaway'. I'm not the sort to fall madly in love, we had a long correspondence about our relationship. I explained that I didn't move at her sort of pace and she said she didn't want to push me. But then I decided that I liked her company, I suppose you could say I fell in love with her and I knew I wasn't likely to meet anyone I'd love more. So with a reasonable offer of a good wife – why not? We were very happy for many years until she died.

Prof. Brian Reddaway, born 1913

Many Marriages

I go to Soham Village College and I hope to become an apprentice for

The High Street, Soham, 1900.

Ethel and Raymond Law in Great Yarmouth, 1965.

computer work. I live with my mother and stepfather, and have younger siblings, they are all stepbrothers and sisters. I'm the only child of my own parents, I have eight half-brothers and thirteen half-sisters scattered about. My mum remarries and then they become my relatives. My mother has been married seven times, my father five times.

John Booth, born 1983

Change of Mind

There's a crucifix on the wall, my wife Ethel likes that sort of thing but it's not for me. Ethel was in a moped accident, she crashed into a lorry that stopped suddenly, she's in a wheelchair now, and she can't move or speak. I have to do everything for her. I prayed when she had her accident, once I wished she'd gone straight away, but I changed my mind as she got better.

Raymond Law, born 1938

Takes Time

I met my wife in Great Paxton; we used to take the same bus. She was more involved in the arty hippie type group of students, but it was later when we were both involved in amateur dramatics that we got together. I was more involved from the technical point of view, like doing the lighting. I didn't like my wife when I first met her, but because I was living in Great Paxton and working in Huntingdon it was easier to stay in Huntingdon on drama workshop days. One day she invited me back for an evening meal, and from there our relationship grew. We're both fairly outward going, like-minded. Her job brings her into contact with the public, she was good fun to be with, and we had a laugh, we just got on well. I fell in love over a period of time; it was my wife who realised first that there was more between us.

Andrew Kendon, born 1957

Violence

When Jayne my daughter was born my husband wasn't there, Jayne had toxaemia. It was only shortly before the birth they did an X-ray and realised that I wasn't expecting one baby but two, twins. The boy had died, but my ex-husband doesn't accept, has never accepted, that we had two children. I

Sandra Wells and her first daughter, Jayne, 1970s.

came home from hospital, the house was filthy, and I cried my eyes out. Things got worse and worse, he got very violent, very physical. We stayed together until Jayne was seven. Sometimes he would hit me, smack me in the mouth, one time I had to go to hospital.

Jayne's life has been in turmoil, from the age of fourteen she's tried to commit suicide because she was bullied at school because the children thought she was spoilt, because she had two sets of parents, she couldn't cope. She left home at fifteen and stayed with the grandparents for a while.

Sandra Wells, born 1955

Kissing

I learned from my sister what girls were, it came naturally. I kissed some girls,

47

the first one was called Gwen, it was in the lobby, I was thirteen, and it was natural. I kissed the policeman's daughter; it was a proper kiss. My sister taught me how to kiss, it was natural, because we liked each other, and it wasn't sexual at all, just brother and sister. Gwen was just a mate, nothing special, just friendly, and in the same class.

Geoffrey Allgood, born 1913

Give and Take

I knew my third husband when I was still married to the second, and when I divorced, he told me he'd loved me all

Mr and Mrs Chown on their wedding day, 26 April 1947.

along and he left his wife for me. We came to live together and married a few years later. We have our differences; it works by give and take. He's a slow and ponderous Fenman while I'm the opposite, but our love is so deep, and he's so kind, that it works.

Billie Bridgement, born 1935

A Kind Man

I met my husband when I worked at St Ives, he would bike after me, then I took him home to see my parents. He'd seen me on the road somewhere. He was a farm worker; he would go down the fens to work, with horses. We used to go for bike rides, there wasn't much entertainment, but we went to Murkett's cinema in Huntingdon. Sometimes we'd bike across the fields, but there was no intercourse. We married in 1935. He asked me to marry him and we did, at Wyton church. I had hesitated about marrying because I loved my parents, but I loved him too, so I decided I would marry him. He died last January; I don't regret any of our life together. I liked him at first, then I grew to love him as I got to know him, he was kind.

Emily Upchurch, born 1915

A Person

My husband is educated, in a good trade, and has a fantastic personality. He's black (Afro-Caribbean), and was adopted as a baby and brought up by a policeman and his wife. He was adopted from a children's home. He joined the Army when he was

Linton High Street, *c.* 1910.

sixteen or seventeen. I was in the Territorial Army; he was attached to the TA unit when I was there. In the last two months he asked me out. We got married when he was in Colchester, and we had a daughter and then we went to America. I married my husband because he had a lovely personality, he didn't drink or smoke and he was understanding and kind. Money didn't matter that much, nor good looks because that they don't last forever, not that he's not good-looking. When I met him I didn't see a colour difference; I'm not black and not white. He's black. When I met him I just saw a person.

Louella Prince, born 1961

Dating Agency

I reached the age of twenty-nine and worried that I'd be left on the shelf. I wasn't meeting anybody socially, and the men at work were all wimps. I saw an advert for the Christian Introductory Service and thought why not? You had to send off a questionnaire; a brother and sister ran it. I decided that if I were going to meet a man it had to be a fellow-Christian. I sent off my details, waited ages, then eventually got a letter saying they'd paired me up.

We got in touch by phone, and talked for hours. We found out we had lots of things in common, and knew the same people. We arranged to meet and I was to wear a red carnation, the classic! We were to meet at the George, and when I walked in, all the waiters and waitresses were wearing red carnations!

He had warned me that part of his face was paralysed, but when I met him, he was so handsome and I was so smitten that I didn't even notice for ages that he had this problem; we were engaged within ten weeks and married five months later. We were very much

49

Huntingdon Street, St Neots, 1910.

A Mepal shop in 1910.

Raymond and Ethel Law's wedding photograph, 6 December 1969.

in love, but he died from a brain tumour, and I still miss him.

Judy Fox, born 1955

Everything Together

I remember meeting my husband, I went to meet a friend on Parker's Piece in 1991 and we met by chance. He spoke to me, he asked me when the music for a festival was coming on and it went from there, our first date was when he cooked me a meal. He was out of work but cooked me an amazing meal, Indian, with spices, tuna, and rice.

We did everything together. We met

in July, bought our present house in August and he asked me to marry him on Christmas Eve.

Lynne Hester, born 1960

Marriage and Independence

Early in my marriage I was living with someone for the first time, I'd always been independent, but I was ill, and suddenly I couldn't even go to the bathroom on my own, and physically needed someone, that was extremely hard to accept. It was moving for me to find out that I could rely on Ted in the way I could. Our first wedding anniversary was really something to celebrate, I'd really been afraid marriage would squash me. I had been terribly ill, and had been in bed for months. I could cycle before I could walk. I remember cycling in France and seeing bright red poppies and just crying, thinking it was so beautiful, my body was repairing itself. I felt so lucky and thankful, it was important too in terms of realising it was okay to depend on someone.

Molly Andrews, born 1959

Cold Dinner

I met my husband when he came into the shop. We went to Young Farmers together, we had a happy courtship, and eventually got married. I'd previously seen him about the town, so I was pleased to be asked out. We went to Cambridge on our first date, and it was the time when Berni Inns were all the fashion, things were nervous and we had fish and chips, he said 'my chips are cold' but I said mine weren't. He called the waitress who pointed out that my chips weren't cold, and I felt I had let him down. I can recall a trip we made to see an aunt, we dressed up and went in a borrowed car. We saw some boys in T-shirts and jumpers and raced them, the police pulled us over and because my husband had his suit on they let him go but penalised the others.

Diana Philipott, born 1951

Alone

Having Kyle has caused problems in a number of relationships I've had because we've been alone for so long he resents anyone that comes between us, and if they tell him off I won't have it, 'he's my son, not yours'; I tell him off, not a man. If you've been brought up with both parents it's different.

Donna Mawby, born 1967

Travelling

I married a man from Bridgwater in Somerset. We used to have a big cooking pot when we travelled, and a big kettle. We travelled in caravans with horses, lots of horses, I liked to see different people, different counties. Evesham was a big place for fruit picking. We met in Sussex when we worked on neighbouring farms. He asked me to marry him, then he came over to ask my father.

Louise Loveridge, born 1914

Late Developer

The boyfriend thing didn't hit me for a long time, not until my A Levels. I was a late developer in many ways. When I was eleven/twelve my parents divorced and I lived with my father and brother, we had to work out a system in the house. I didn't start to grow up until university. My first date was when I was sixteen. I was working in a shop as a Saturday girl, one of the boys from school in my year he asked me to go the pictures to see *Platoon*. He was called Robert. I haven't had many serious boyfriends; I'm now on number two.

My father remarried five years ago; it's nice to see him finding happiness again.

Hemingford Abbotts in the 1950s.

My mother has died but had several partners before then, but she never remarried.

Laura Hunt, born 1974

Coming Out

I wear a ribbon which is a gay symbol. My first affair was about two years ago. I ended it because I realised I didn't love or trust him. I couldn't trust him with secrets. If I have another boyfriend it has to be someone I can trust and be close to. The boyfriend adored me though he didn't love me. But he wouldn't marry; I would like to marry another man.

Edward Venni, born 1974

Isleham

I met my wife Olive in the nearby village of Isleham. She was working for a dressmaker making MA hoods in Cambridge. She lived at Hilton where she belonged to the Baptist church, while I belonged to the Baptist church in Soham. In Isleham there used to be annual rallies for young people with a special speaker, one of these was an ex-naval man.

She'd lost a brother on a submarine in the war. She decided to hear the speaker, and her friend took her to Isleham. My nephew and I also went there and we began corresponding. Then we met in Cambridge and that was the beginning of the courtship. I didn't fall in love straight away. I was a bit indifferent, but then we got to know

Queen Street in Peterborough with a woman pushing what looks, now, like an ancient pram, 1900.

each other. I chose her because all my young days I'd moved from home to home, when father died I had to go and live with a brother. Then I went from one brother or sister to another. Babies were being born, and each time this happened I had to move. When one brother told me that he too was expecting a baby, I got fed up and asked Olive to marry me. We married a few months later; it's our fiftieth anniversary tomorrow.

John Martin, born 1926

Cycling Love Affair

One day at the fair I saw a girl, and my brother said 'are you going to treat her on the dodgems?' I said 'no' and my brother said 'if you don't I shall', so I did. She rushed off and I didn't see her for a week. She was working in a pub, living at home, and later she went to work for a parson, as a domestic, I had a job cycling twenty-six miles to Sutton to see her. There was a postman's job going near us at Burnt Fen, so she took the job and came to live with my family. My stepmother said we should get married to stop people talking, so we did, and after the war we got a council house.

Harry Bye, born 1917

Dancing

There was an older man living near us who said there was a social dance

John Martin, Christmas, 1983.

and he'd walk me down there. There was snow on the ground and two planks across the brook. The dance was held in a schoolroom, which smelled of paraffin. No one asked me to dance, but I was used to that from London, to dancing with women because there were no men, so when I went again I made up my mind not to just sit for three hours again.

The next time I got up and asked another girl to dance. None of the men would dance and one man I spoke to said 'I pay my money to see people like you make fools of themselves'. When it was time to go home the others had all left, I asked someone if there was a boy to walk me home and in the dark a male voice said 'I'll walk with you'. I couldn't see him. I could only see his feet and thought his shoes need blacking. He told me all about himself, he worked as a thatcher. I thought he sounded

Harry Bye, in his cycling days, in the 1930s.

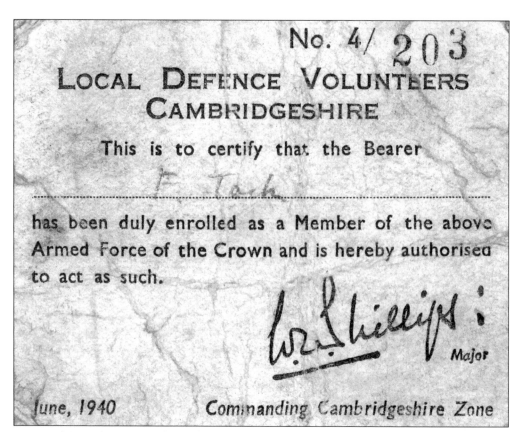

No. 4/ 2 0 3

LOCAL DEFENCE VOLUNTEERS CAMBRIDGESHIRE

This is to certify that the Bearer

.... F Tack ....

has been duly enrolled as a Member of the above Armed Force of the Crown and is hereby authorised to act as such.

W.E.Phillips:

Major

June, 1940   Commanding Cambridgeshire Zone

Frank Tack's Home Guard Certificate.

intelligent and interesting. When I got in my mother asked who had walked me home, but I had no idea. I went to thank the woman who'd arranged for her son to take me home, we sat drinking tea, then he offered to take me home again and it was the young man who's spoken to me scathingly at the dance!

Later we joked about it all, and we got engaged. I waited to marry until I was twenty-one, because I knew my father wouldn't approve. He didn't think my husband was good enough, eventually my father agreed to sign the marriage consent form. He told me never to ask for anything again, he would have nothing to do with my husband, and anything I had from his home to my home, a price would be put on it and I would have to pay for it. My mother had to make a list and we paid everything off over weeks and weeks. We thought he might not come to the wedding to give me away, so we had alternative arrangements, but he did come. Everything was so expensive I couldn't have the white dress I'd saved up for.

Dora Tack, born 1921

Ignorant about Sex

I learnt about sex from my husband; making love for the first time aged seventeen. I met him in the chocolate factory where I worked. When we were courting I had to be home at ten o'clock at night. We married after six months. People married for affection and showed affection more. People didn't separate then, I stayed with my husband until he died. We both knew what we wanted, to be a normal couple with children.

Alice Humm, born 1893

Right from Wrong

Relationships in my family were loving, we were taught right from wrong, I respected my parents, they taught us (the children) to care for each other, for the planet, etc. My brother took care of me when we were young, he once gave me two pounds 'to spend wisly' (*sic*). My parents gave me advice on contraception, but they didn't interfere, they were very broad-minded. Once, a man I knew, a platonic acquaintance, stayed the night and my parents simply asked in the morning 'one cup of coffee or two?'

Sally Scott, born 1965

Hiding the Truth

My sister and I weren't very close, my sister was my mum's favourite and I was my aunt's. Later when I went to work at the GPO in Huntingdon I lived with my aunt in Godmanchester which was nearer, she was like a mother to me, that's how close we were. I think my aunt was trying to make up to me what she didn't do for my mother. You see it was an 'upstairs-downstairs story'. I later

found out that my mother was really my 'aunt's' daughter, not her sister; my aunt had worked in domestic service and had been seduced by her boss's son. She became pregnant and went away to have the baby, and when she came back she arranged to have the child brought up by other people. The child was passed off as her sister instead of her daughter. So really she was my grandmother and not my aunt at all. If people had known she had had an illegitimate child by her boss's son, she would have been sacked. In those days it was always the girl who took the blame for such things.

Lillian Melton, born 1932

Harry Tack in his Army uniform.

Mill Road, Romsey, 1978.

Not Worthy

My husband and I had a very happy marriage. He was poor but loved having a home, he was the son of an artist and a neurotic arts student, and never had any money and granny would never invite anybody home because she was embarrassed. She was a rotten organiser and a worse cook and she'd sit in a corner with her hands folded thinking beautiful thoughts. I thought it romantic and pre-Raphaelite to start with, but later she came to stay with us during the war and she'd sit with her hands folded and it never occurred to her to help at all. She thought I was a husky Yorkshire girl not worthy of her son, and we had a difficult relationship. I was critical of her but I also felt sorry for the frail old lady who was much older than my mother was.

Margo Bullman, born 1913

Brother's Girlfriend

After the war ended people wanted to marry and get on with their lives. People had become less static than before the war. My wife and I had been at the same school, she had been my brother's girlfriend before the war, then he was killed and I took his place in her life. Previously I had another girlfriend, but she got involved with an American while I was away.

Norman Pentelow, born 1922

58

CHAPTER **4**

Crime and law

Richard Carter's police photograph, 1978. Richard is in the back row, in the middle.

Fateful Saturday Night

My daughter Jayne formed a relationship with man called Darren, it lasted for about two years, and they split June this year. Darren was stalking Jayne for about three months and trying to get back with her.

Then one night in September they met in the street, argued and he beat Jayne up in the street and followed her to her house, they had an argument in the house, and unfortunately Jayne stabbed him. I died then, a bit of me died in the way I felt. Jayne was put into prison for the first week, it was the most horrendous time of my life. Even three months later I'm still very tearful about it.

Jayne's boyfriend systematically wore her down. I didn't believe her to begin with because Jayne told me so many lies. Once she'd stabbed him and been to prison I saw what she was like, it was as if someone had taken a curtain off my eyes. When someone hurts you as she had done, you put up a barrier, you don't want to see the truth, and you just want to hide behind the barrier. Then I saw how thin she'd got and I realised things Jayne had told me were true. Darren had been involved with drugs and kept Jayne short of money and had no food, I thought she was lying, I had food and money and refused to give her money. Then I realised how little Jayne weighed, I'd noticed it but hadn't noticed – I didn't really realise until I saw her in prison. We got her out on bail.

Sandra Wells with her two daughters, Jayne and Hannah.

I put up every penny I had in cash to get Jayne out, so did my ex-husband. It was the worst week of my life, something died, the old relationship with Denis my ex-husband, and my relationship with Jayne. Once Jayne got bail it was as if something new was happening, and now it's changing. Now it's a lot better relationship than I could ever have hoped for, Jayne is living with my parents. Denis and I ferry her back and forth to solicitors. Denis and I share the care of Alanah her daughter, it's as if every time I'm there for her. We can now spend hours talking and we don't end up rowing, whereas before after fifteen minutes I would want to throttle her. It took this to make things change. I agree with my mother that in many ways your life is mapped out for you, it's your destiny, it's going to happen.

Sandra Wells, born 1955

Attacks on the Elderly

People have this idea that elderly people are vulnerable to violent attacks, but in all my years as a police officer, I've not been to more than two or three such incidents. I remember an incident in which I had to break into the house of an old woman that hadn't been heard from for a long time. We found cash all around the house, plus an automatic pistol and ammunition hidden up the chimney which someone had given her, this is one of the most unusual things I've seen hidden in someone's house.

Richard Carter, born 1955

Everything Upside Down

The police are always raiding our caravan site. They turn everything upside down, even if you're completely innocent they're liable to turn all your possessions over. On my brother's birthday there was raid, there were presents that never got unwrapped (except by the police), the police checked everything, they verbally abused people, made people lie on the floor with a gun at their heads; there'll never be good relations between gypsies and the police.

Charmayne Mercer, born 1978

Like Me

I went to Norwich Prison for training to become a prison officer. There I met a prisoner whom I knew from my childhood: we were at the same school; we recognised each other. At breakfast I went up to his table, but in 1974 you couldn't talk to a prisoner, it was starting to change, but it was still the dark ages – they couldn't talk to you and you couldn't talk to them. I went up to him because he was a friend, he had a nice personality and was similar to me, dragged up on a council estate like me. I got a rollicking for talking to him, and learned a lesson from that. I waited and went to talk to him later, and it was like the *Porridge* programme on television, 'have you got a fag?' etc. He's since died, died of a heart attack while committing a burglary.

John Bennett-Collins, born 1945

Celery planting at Burnt Fen, 1940s.

Prison Visit

It was horrendous going to visit Jayne in prison, they treat you like a criminal, even though she was only on remand and in the eyes of the law you're innocent until proven guilty. I had a sick feeling walking in there, they stamp your hands and you're not allowed to take anything in with you. You have to leave everything in a locker, you're searched, you're not allowed to cuddle them, you're made to feel like a convict yourself, they're not allowed off a square piece of carpet. We weren't allowed to give Jayne any money, you're locked in with them, it made me feel sick and angry that they treated Jayne like that when she hadn't been convicted. It was horrible to think she was so far away, but then she got bail, and had to report to the police every day, except on Christmas Day! The charge was attempted murder, but it was scaled down, and eventually she just got probation.

Sandra Wells, born 1955

The Birch

On the farm there was a young man who'd been in prison for stealing from the shops in Ely, the third time they gave him the birch and he said he would never steal again, and he never did! It was the pain and humiliation.

John Martin, born 1926

Motorbike

When I was a prison officer and met a prisoner I'd known as a child, I thought how strange it was we'd ended up on opposite sides of the law. Once I was banned from driving: I used to scramble a motorbike and take it down to the road when I was fourteen – I got caught and taken to juvenile court. My mother was in court: they fined me £13 and banned me from driving for three months. But my mother told the magistrate she couldn't afford to pay the fine, and would have to pay 10s a month. That was what turned me, perhaps otherwise I could have been a criminal, it was a watershed. I thought what a prat I was, putting my parents – especially my mother – through it. I owned up to it when I applied to the prison service.

John Bennett-Collins, born 1945

Abused

I was born in Liverpool into a large family, six brothers, four sisters, we lived in a council house, father worked nights. I used to run away from home because of fear, my father was violent. I was sent away because my parents couldn't cope, I was sent to a special school, a boarding school, for

Saturday crowds, outside the Peterborough Corn Exchange on Church Street.

maladjusted children. Some of my brothers were also sent away because of the abuse at home. The abuse was verbal, physical and sexual. But I was abused again in the special school.

When I was fifteen, I was sent to prison for three years. I was terrified, it was dark and cold, I was taken to a cell and the door was slammed, it was my first time in prison and I was in shock, I was crying, I wanted to tell someone what had happened to me but I couldn't, everything was grey and bleak. The officers never spoke, they all shouted and screamed, that was very intimidating, at night I had a terrible nightmare and woke up screaming, but no-one came. The next day I was woken by somebody screaming. I was fifteen and in an adult prison, when I went to recess the stench was overwhelming, there was no sanitation, only pots. An officer threw a razor blade into my cell and told me to shave. I had missed breakfast but was given a mug of tea and someone told me to drink half of it and use the other half to shave with. I had never shaved in my life and I was cut to bits because nobody had ever taught me how to. You had no choice, you had to shave.

I've taken an SOTP (Sexual Offenders Therapy) course in Littlehey prison, about victim empathy, seeing the victim's perspective, role-play as a victim. You're dealing with your own pain, you have to sort that out first, to understand what happened and why, then you start feeling. When you harm someone, you cut the pain off, you shut off from it, you close down, you feel you can't cope, you feel you'll end it all if you look at the pain. Suicide does run in your mind, even as a youngster, you

build walls and barriers over the years, and no-one can get in, you learn to use physical force and barriers. The role-play was a turning point, it made me realise the gravity of my offending. I played the victim's part and I felt a deep revulsion for the person that was playing me. I wish I could turn the clock back, I'd like to say sorry to my victims, but it's not enough. The only way I can show my feelings is by taking these courses, to show I'm atoning for what I did. Whatever happens, even if I'm never released, I'll have a better quality of life, because of the courses I've done at Littlehey. Nothing had ever touched me until I came here, they don't let you forget what you put your victim through, no-one has the right to offend against any other human being. I took an innocent person's life, I got a life sentence. I had no right to take another person's life.

Joe Ronan, born 1946

CHAPTER 5

Growing up

A fete in Eaton Socon (St Neots), 1910.

Weetabix

We were very poor and couldn't afford things. Once my mother asked me what I wanted for Christmas and I said 'a big packet of Weetabix and a bottle of milk to myself.' When I was born it was so easy she nearly had me in the taxi on the way to the hospital. I now have two children and I can't imagine how my mother coped. People are more worried now, but there were weird and wonderful people when I was a boy, the Bradys, the Moors murderers.

Brian Pearce, born 1949

Pheasants

When we came to the Fens it seemed to me a unique thing that you could go out all day. We'd make bows and arrows, try to catch pheasants, rabbits, we had air rifles. No-one seemed to be bothered – you couldn't imagine that today, could you, a fourteen year old walking around with a gun? In the summer in the harvest it was fantastic, in the haystacks, trespassing on farms and fields. I used to catch pike with a spear. We'd get a pitchfork and break off one tine, then put the other into the water and spear the pike. We didn't catch many rabbits, they're quick, but we hit pheasants with catapults, or at night we'd just grab them – break their necks, make a fire, strip off the feathers, and cook them. My parents weren't unduly concerned about where we were – we'd tell them where we were going, or I'd lie, say I'd be at a friend's house when in fact I was out on the fields, acting daft. There wasn't the fear that parents have these days, of child molesters etc., you could feel safe.

John Bennett-Collins, born 1945

Eleven Plus

I loved the first eleven years of my life, after that, I passed the eleven plus and went to what's now Kimbolton School, then a grammar school, and I didn't enjoy it at all. The school had many boarders and the day boys were regarded as the lowest of the low. We weren't treated well. I remember the prefects, they'd make sure the day boys were last in the queue for lunch, they'd make sure we didn't to talk to teachers and we were punished harder than the others. Prefects were allowed to cane and strap just as the teachers were. It was the feeling of the place. We weren't encouraged to develop our skills.

David Chambers, born 1942

Haircut

I remember wanting my hair cut, my mother was very religious and thought I should keep it long, but when I was twelve I made such a fuss that eventually my mother arranged for a hairdresser to come and cut it. For some reason I cried, my sister Ursula offered to treat me to a perm, I became the first person in school to have a perm. It was a turning point, because I then became popular and a prefect. Then Ursula my sister gave me some make up and I turned from an ugly duckling into a swan.

Iris Crossley, born 1924

Iris Crossley (middle) on the beach, 1933.

St Neots

Peterborough was so different from St Neots, which didn't even have a cinema. I remember my first visit to the cinema with a 'boyfriend' when I was ten, but during my teenage years I had long schooldays, then I had homework, then I had to work to earn money to supplement the income. So going to Peterborough was liberation, being able to do things without always having to say when I'd be in, even though my parents were quite liberal. I remember going to a nightclub in Peterborough: you'd sit with a soft drink all evening because you were driving. The soft drinks cost more than the alcohol, because they wanted you to buy alcohol.

Judy Fox, born 1955

Mother Left

My parents separated in 1952, mother went off, I didn't know where she was for fourteen years, I did find her in the end. My father married again, and then had another family. There were arguments when I was a child, more or less on my mother's side, she was very vocal, and she could pick things up and throw, but that was something we were used to. You'd see the arguing, but you didn't think it meant anything, it was a way of life, you never thought that they would ever part, that didn't even come into your mind because it was something that wasn't done. Being a small village, when she did go people used to point and say 'they're the children that the mother's walked off and left', because it was something that wasn't done, not even for fathers to go. One Saturday morning we came back and my father turned round and said 'your mother's gone', and that was it. We just accepted it, it was funny really, she was gone, life started getting harder, in the respect that we didn't have a mother to look after us, but at home things were also calmer, there wasn't the aggression there any more so you felt at peace, really. It was an improvement. My father came home and there was a letter there, it was my twelfth birthday the next day and she'd left me two shillings' worth of marbles, because it was the marble time, for my birthday, and that was it. Just a letter to say she'd gone. She left with somebody that at one point was our lodger, she stayed with him until he died. My father didn't know they were having a relationship. Dad got on with his work, he went to the post office, it

was worrying for him because he did a shift where one week in three had to be nights, when he had to meet the train and take the other mail down. So we had to have grandfather come in and look after us those nights – he used to frighten us a bit, because in those days there used to be a saying that if there was thunder and lightning you covered all the mirrors up, and you weren't allowed to have needles and scissors on a Sunday because it was bad luck, and he used to frighten us, so father had to try and get housekeepers, but they never seemed to want to take responsibility for long. So in the end, my stepmother came to stop us going in a home, which was just about due to happen, because father couldn't keep his work in the post office and keep us all together, and he wanted us all together. So that saved us going in a home, and she stayed with my father for forty years, until he died.

Grace Robinson, born 1940

Tomboy

I was a tomboy, I played with three boys, the butchers' sons, we had a den and made go-karts for ourselves, we played on swings too. The men in the shop would help me. I was mainly with men, the police, and men in the brewery nearby. I had dolls and a doll's pram, but also a train set that was my favourite toy. I made villages out of kits for the trains to go through, and I had Dinky toys and there was spray-on grass, I enjoyed that train set.

Diana Philipott, born 1951

A young Diana Philpott, 1950s or '60s.

Rebel

My father and I used to argue a lot, we're both alike and look alike with red hair.

When I was thirteen or so, I rebelled. Once we had a big argument and he threatened to hit me, he did hit me and I hit him back and broke his nose. I never hit him again, now we joke about it. In those days being smacked was part of growing up. Once he used his belt when I was naughty, he used to say 'come home at 7.30'. I'd wind my watch back and it would say 6.30 when it was 7.30; I used to get into trouble and being hit did me no harm, it made me have respect, he was right. My mother hit me, but only very rarely.

Sandra Wells, born 1955

Quite Tough

We moved to a new council housing estate in Cherry Hinton, a village just outside Cambridge. We moved from a flat, to this new post-war housing estate in 1952. I was two, but I can remember that the back garden was facing onto yellow cornfields. They had little cottages in the High Street then, and they drove tractors and livestock through the village. My parents were part of that generation who had been in the war, the so-called 'New Elizabethans'. This was their first house, and all of these kinds of families moved in together, at the same time. All the kids grew up together, and played together in the streets. The parents mostly got on with each other, but for the children it could be quite a tough environment, although not as tough as an inner city of course. As an only child I felt a bit vulnerable, because I had no brothers and sisters to call on if I got into conflict with other kids. One day at this primary school, I got into a row with another boy in the cloakroom, and when I came home, I had scratches and bruises across my face. My mother was outraged and wanted to go to the school, but I stopped her from doing that, because I would have been ashamed if she had taken my part. So I learned to be more watchful.

Paul Crossley, born 1950

Chatteris

I remember the hobble skirt coming in, then the peg skirt. I wondered how women got on and off the buses with a hobble skirt. I used to pull my skirts up to look younger to attract the boys, skirts were so heavy and long we had brush-braid on the bottom, to protect the hem.

I was twelve when the First World War broke out. I remember the boys enlisting, one after the other. I made comforts at school – knitting for the troops, socks and scarves, and other things to keep them warm. All my brothers enlisted and they all were wounded: one was repairing a telegraph pole, and there was a shell which burst, it split the wire and came back in his eye, it cut his eye out. He fell down and at the same time there was a gas attack, so he was gassed. He didn't die then but he always had breathing problems after that. He got a wonderful pension: thirteen shillings and ninepence a

Sam Allgood, Geoffrey's father, on a binding machine at harvest time, 1920s.

week! Actually it was meagre, and then he had to have a means test. After a few years, in 1925, he died of consumption. My youngest brother was a runner in the trenches, and got shot in the arm: he got a medal for delivering messages under fire.

Meg Tuck, born 1902

Working with Cars

My first job was at the Royston Motor Co. I had to be there at 8, I got there early, but no one else arrived until 8.20. First I had to wash the floor, then I'd got to clean the car engine, that's how I learned how they worked. We did cars for all sorts of people, including rich Indians. I started work in 1928. Later they employed people under me, so I lost the most menial jobs. I built myself into a good mechanic.

Geoffrey Allgood, born 1913

Coal Fires

When I was young we had coal fires and fenders, later we got more open fires and a scullery with a copper: You lit the fire under it, mostly on Mondays, to do the washing. Washing was very hard work, children helped, everything in the house was hard. There were no labour-saving devices, no carpets, only lino and rugs, the bedrooms were very cold.

Dorothy Grubb, born 1908

Comberton

Comberton was a good, run-of-the-mill, average school. I was once bullied at school but I hit back. I bullied people, especially one boy in the village, he was a neighbour, a cheeky chappy. If he annoyed me, then I would bully him and hide his skates etc. Sometimes I would shun the boy so that he had no

70

one to play with. It wasn't really bullying, it was just because he annoyed me, he wouldn't cry, he'd just go off. I didn't dislike him. I regret bullying anyone, but at that time it was a natural thing to do, kids do that. Now the boy works for Amnesty International.

Duncan Baines, born 1973

Village School

There were hardly any cars around, and you could play without being afraid of being run down. You chalked wickets on a gate and played cricket, you played tag games, both boys and girls, until well into the evening when our mothers would come out and call us in for supper. The village school was packed with children when I went, completely overflowing. It seemed they weren't ready for the expansion in the village, and the junior school for the seven to elevens wasn't ready until the mid-'50s. You seemed to get lost amongst all those children, you felt you were just one of a huge crowd and you could easily be left behind in terms of learning. In that respect I was lucky, because I had a wonderful teacher called Bertha Rush, who found out one day that I had been there for nine months and nobody was teaching me to read. She picked me and a small group of others out, and started to work vigorously with us so that we would meet the standards, and surpass them. It was really down to her that I

Friends of Dorothy Grubb on a coach outing, 1926.

Eric Nicholson

started writing and composing essays and poems.

Paul Crossley, born 1950

Impersonator

I used to stammer when I was a boy. One day in the schoolyard when I was about ten, I had a group of boys around me and one of the teachers walked past, then turned round and stopped. He had overheard me imitating another teacher and said, 'come back with me'. I thought I was in dire trouble. He said, 'why is it I can't get a word out of you in class, and yet I distinctly heard the voice of Mr Morrison coming out of your mouth and there was no stammer?' I explained to him – with a stammer – that I could be anybody else but myself. The teacher said 'all right then, when you come to my class in future, you be whoever you want to be'. And so from then on, whenever I went to class, I was always someone else – someone I'd heard on stage, for example, or the man next door. That's how I was able to speak without a stammer. Hiding behind other people. It was the beginnings of being an impersonator, that's how I became an actor.

Eric Nicholson, born 1925

Village Life

I didn't know where some of the neighbouring villages were, people didn't travel, the changes in the village were slow. Now, there's hardly anyone living in the village who still works there, apart from those who work from home on computers. When I was a child you worked in agriculture or on the railway, there were two gangs on the railway. Things changed dramatically when people all went from the village to work and saw a broader world than they'd been used to.

When I was young it was purely an agricultural village, nobody was rich. The farmer was not much better off than those who worked for him were. Sixty acres was considered big. The village was dirty in the winter and it was difficult to ride a bike to the railway because of the sugar beet and cows on the road, it was messy. When I was younger I always hoped there would be some change for the better, and that is why later I supported the village's expansion which other people opposed.

John Taylor, born 1932

Hot Water

During the war I ran the office for Bidwells (a land and estate agents and auctioneers) in Ipswich. I remember lorries waiting to move off for D-Day, and the doodlebug. I also remember coming to Grantchester, and floors being taken up to put in electricity. We had central heating and a coke boiler from 1922 to '62. Then we got oil, and now it's gas. I washed infrequently in hot water and at school we just had a jug and bowl.

Anthony Pemberton, born 1942

School Days

In school you had to sit according to your place in the alphabet, I sat by a window, far from the heat, and always had chilblains. We had to walk to school, but we were content with less, for example with a whip top, marbles, hoops, we played hopscotch and we used to sing various songs in our breaks. There was a lot of playing together, and there was a neighbourly spirit. At Xmas we got one present and a stocking with an orange, an apple and a tangerine at the bottom.

Later I used to go to the workhouse with children from the Sunday school, they were very austere buildings, and the old ladies and gentlemen were separated,

couples who'd lived together for years. It was very sad, the only thing they were allowed to receive from us was peppermints, so we always used to take bags of peppermints along to give them.

Dorothy Grubb, born 1908

Embarrassed

Once a boy in my class, when I was only about five, a boy called John Thomas, was hauled in front of all the children and spanked for being cheeky. It made me aware that if you weren't careful, you could be made to feel embarrassed and ashamed very quickly. I realised that punishment was part of the school world; I accepted it.

Paul Crossley, born 1950

Dorothy Grubb in holiday attire, 1920s.

Evacuee

I came to the Fens as an evacuee aged five. I came on the train, it was very cold. I remember climbing on the pipes to keep warm, I wet myself and got very dirty. My sister was more attractive and pristine. We were taken to Doddington school to be chosen for fostering, boys got taken first because they could help on farms, pretty girls second, nobody wanted me because I was so mucky and plain. My sister was chosen and insisted that I go with her. We were so lucky to get wonderful foster-parents, our parents stayed in London although the docks were very dangerous. It was heartbreaking going back, my foster-parents were cultured, and had aspirations, nice cups and saucers. I went back to a bombed-out home and we had thick cups, I felt sick and resented my parents, I resented not having nice things. It was not their fault they couldn't get things. Many years later I discussed it with my parents and resented myself for resenting them! My foster-parents had a smallholding, they kept pigs and we used to eat pigs' brains on toast. It sounds awful but it was wonderful, we ate all the bits other people didn't want. I worked, I had a paper round. We went home with £24, which our foster-parents had saved for us.

Billie Bridgement, born 1935

Farmyard

My parents were lovely, my father was a land worker and worked for a Mr Johnson at Oldhurst, they had a

Doddington High Street, 1930s.

The old bridge, Huntingdon, 1929.

big farmyard with cows and horses. I was one of three, we had a lovely time, when I was four years old we had a tin tea service with rose buds. We used to take them under the trees, fill them with water and pretend it was tea. I had lovely dolls. We never wanted for anything, for food. If dad was at work, mum would take a wicker basket out to him in the harvest fields, he loved cheese, and I love it too. If we had a mid-day meal we would take that out to him too.

Emily Upchurch, born 1915

Helping Mother

The best thing in my life was schooldays. When I was twelve or thirteen, the schoolmaster used to tell me it was time to go home and get my mother a drink at eleven o'clock.

Mother had a small baby, and he said it was my job to go and help her. So I would leave school, go home and get my mother a milk drink, and then return to school.

Gladys Bateman, born 1909

Ice Skating

I remember skating on the Great Lake at Windsor Park, it was a very cold winter. There was ice in the wash bowls when we woke up. Everything had to go on the bed to keep warm, such as overcoats. There was no central heating. I remember Eton, it is a less harsh regime now, but then there was a lot of bullying and corporal punishment. Then we accepted it as the norm. I had my share of beatings.

Anthony Pemberton, born 1942

Learning to Speak

I went to speech therapy from age three or four. I had a fishing rod with a magnet on, and a picture as part of the therapy; it was to make teaching fun. I also remember my reading books. 'A' for Apple, 'R' for Robber etc., and stories. It's good to go to school, because if you didn't, you wouldn't learn, and then you wouldn't get a job easily when you grow up.

Syringa Fox, born 1989

Playing

When I was a child my mother was always there at home. She put blankets over the table for us to play under, and would take us for walks.

Richard Carter, born 1955

Losing my Sight

I was a shy quiet child and the grown-ups' attitude to me was bewildering. I was losing my sight and I became more aware of my condition when I was about seven and children would accuse me of staring. My mother was worried, and was always testing me. People would ask her in the street how I was and say it was a great pity: I hated that. My brother also lost his sight, but not until he was eleven. And then he had to go to a special school, that was a greater shock, more sudden.

Lynne Hester, born 1960

Too Tall

I was tall for my age so they had to buy new furniture, a new desk, because I couldn't fit under the ones that were there. Then I began to learn, once I had glasses, a new desk, and a new teacher. The school was tiny, like the village, the other teacher was the only one, and she carried on as she had done many years before. I had to be carried to school, I absolutely hated it, and it has since been closed.

Linda Hill, born 1961

March

I went to Neal Wade Comprehensive School in March. I visited it the other day, and it seems to be dropping off now, it's happening all over the country. I look at some of the things my brother gets up to, and if I had done that when I was starting there I'd have been sent out. The discipline seems to have gone down a lot. There's now so little a teacher can do that things are running out of control. When I started off, you had to stand up every time a teacher came into a room; that's gone now. Also the language you can get away with now, it's certainly coarser than what I remember, I'm not sure why this is.

Gavin Philpott, born 1980

Away at School

I went to prep school at age seven. At first I minded, but not later. We had our own rooms and had to work a lot in our own time, and it taught us to organize our own lives. We didn't think about our parents or missing them, everybody was in the same boat.

Anthony Pemberton, born 1942

Anorexia

I was very ill when I was twenty-one. I had anorexia and it was only my nan who helped me and made sure there was food I could eat even if I didn't and she took me to the doctor's. My mum couldn't cope, my nan couldn't either but she tried. The doctor had to tell them what was wrong. It started when I had a boyfriend and we went for a meal. Afterwards my stomach was a bit bloated and he said 'you'll have to lose weight or I'll trade you in for a younger model'. It was only a chance remark but after that I wouldn't eat at all, it went from there. I moved into a bedsit and then the bloke and I split up. I got down to four and a half stone, but things have changed so much: now there's lots of help for women in my situation, then the doctor just gave me pills and sent me away.

Donna Mawby, born 1967

Staying with Granny

For most of my school years I stayed with my granny during the week and went back to the farm in the Fens at the weekend and for holidays. I used to play with my sisters and cousins around the farm. There was a big American airbase at Alconbury, during the war there were

Broad Street, March, in the 1920s.

The High Street, Chatteris in the 1960s.

big bombers that would come down, some of them having been shot at, engines not going. They would offload whatever they could, including rubber dinghies that we used to play with. The Americans would give us some, they were very big-hearted. They'd shoot different coloured lights from the planes as signals to show whether there were injured people on board, then we'd play with the lights too.

Terry Huggins, born 1934

Panic

I played with my brother when I was young, sport, cricket, and football. When I got older, my mother was really dependent on me. I remember my mother's panic over open spaces and going on holiday. My brother and I had to do the shopping because she was too scared to go out. It didn't make us more confident, when I was an adolescent, her fears came back to me. My sister found it hard, she left home, married and had children very young, to escape!

Lynne Hester, born 1960

Mistake

I went in for the eleven plus, and made a critical mistake based on how I'd been taught, which meant I didn't finish. I failed, but took it again later that year. It was between one other boy and me and I recall the headmaster telling me they'd given it to the other boy. It was the end of my world. Many years later, I was asked onto the Board of the same school that I'd failed to get into. They assumed I'd been a pupil there, but I told them I hadn't.

Roy Habbin, born 1925

Own Amusement

When we were children we played a game with squares on which we kicked stones, we also played ball games, and cowboys and Indians. We could make lovely bows and arrows from the willow trees, which grew there in plenty. Sometimes we got into mischief, but it was nothing like the violence of now, vandalism. A bike could be left outside unlocked, you can't do that now.

John Martin, born 1926

Living with Grandparents

I grew up in a small community in Ramsey Mereside and worked with my grandfather on the farm from an early age. I spent spells living with my grandparents, and sometimes I used to visit my great-aunt, mainly because she had a television.

We were all working people and felt privileged to move into a council house with a school round the corner. I had two chances to go to a grammar school but already knew I wanted to go into farming, not be academic. I also wanted to continue to play rugby and the grammar school played football!

Brian Abblitt, born 1948

Yarmouth, July 1947. The boys of the Sussex Regiment, from left to right, are: Oliver Peck, Eric Howlett, Peter Kemp, Derek Balls, John Martin.

The wedding of Dora Tack's sister-in-law, December 1941.

Underclothes

It was only when I went to school I found out that everyone didn't wear drawers. I wet my drawers in school and was embarrassed when the others reacted to them when they were taken off.

Dora Tack, born 1921

Boarding School

My father was a fellow of King's College. I went to boarding schools, but was brought up largely in Cambridge. We lived in a large house, with two maids, a cook and a housemaid. We also had a nursemaid until 1920, known as 'Nan', she lived in but left to get married. She had a room upstairs and I was sent there if I was in disgrace, but I got on well with her, she was like a second mother.

Prof. Brian Reddaway, born 1913

Farming

I grew up on a farm. I used to help my father and grandfather on the farm. I remember the harvest and driving tractors, haycarts, hedge-laying. I used to help feed and milk the cows, and prepare the pigswill – the pigs liked it. A college owned the farm, and it was run by a family called the Clarks. My mother used to clean for them, they had a big house. We didn't socialise together but they weren't aloof, the fathers would drink together in the pub sometimes, there was no class divide in that way.

John Hoppett, born 1948

Class Difference

My first serious girlfriend was English. A lot of middle-class people don't think about race but economic standing. You're all right as long as you're clean and smart, whereas working class parents are more inclined to be racist. Professional parents I would get on with, but with working class people it's different, then it was more: 'I don't want my daughter going out with a Paki'.

Waheed Rabbani, born 1970

Seduced

The sister of a friend initiated me into sex, I was twelve, she was sixteen, she was babysitting and I was invited round, it was great, I was gently seduced. It wasn't a full sexual experience, more a fumbling. My friend never knew. I had been told nothing about sex at home or at school.

Colin Warlow, born 1960

Bath Time

We bathed in a tin bath, which you filled, heated, and put on the table in front of the fire. Bath was on a Friday, my parents bathed in privacy but I didn't. I was an only child, I was quite happy then, though I would have liked

The High Street, Histon, 1900.

Lady Fliers at an air circus, Bury St Edmunds in 1933, photographed by Harry Bye.

siblings, but it was a small village and a lot of my friends were also only children.

John Hoppett, born 1948

Young at Heart

I think of myself as young at heart, I don't feel old at all, love having young children around. I realise looking at myself, I'm getting older, there are things I can no longer do, like running around a hockey field. Chasing my granddaughter around brings my age home to me, I don't like the idea of getting old, don't want to be like my father-in-law was. He was a burden, he was active when I first moved in with

him, he had an accident and that is when he started to go downhill. I cared for him, mornings and evenings. Eventually I couldn't cope with him and had to get help. Sadly, he died the same year that our son died.

Sandra Wells, born 1955

Old As You Feel

Age is all in the mind. It makes you realise how quickly life goes. The night before my grandmother died she said it only seemed like yesterday she was at school, I still think about my school. I recall someone bringing a condom to school, I couldn't believe it was a condom because they were made of rubber and the only rubber I knew was on the baby's bed to stop it wetting the mattress. I am from a family of eleven, my mother only wanted six, she told my dad off when they had the last two.

Brian Pearce, born 1949

Fast Pace

The pace of life here is fast, people tear around. In Poland where my family came from, they go at their own pace and enjoy things. For example, when we visited the Tatra mountains we saw that people would just walk, sit, and appreciate and enjoy what's around, they don't have everything there that we have here. Here the media push everything, you have to have everything straight away, but there they don't, they appreciate natural things. Here children would say, 'that's boring', they want the next latest thing, then they chuck it and want something else. My nieces and my friend's children are like that.

Anna Wiseman, born 1949

Age

Growing old is a fact of life, when people get older they get more

Chapel Square, Stretham, 1911.

respect, they're more fragile, they can't do things for themselves. When you get to your thirties, forties, fifties, I'm looking forward to that, because then you've got everything. You've still got half your life left in front of you, but there's nothing ahead of you that's really challenging. I have to think about getting on and going to university, but at that age there won't be any main pressures. We start to get old at about forty-five, fifty; my parents aren't old, my dad's forty-two and my mother is forty-one, they're getting there! But they won't just suddenly get old, they'll start to reduce things and then one day, they'll just start playing bingo! But I don't intend to do that. I hope to keep on enjoying life until I drop dead!

Tim O'Connell, born 1984

First Love

I had no girlfriends, not until I met my wife in 1986. She was my first girlfriend, I had too many other things to do before that. I never thought about sex at all, I was too busy with other things. I left school, then did GSEs, then 'O' Levels, and an art 'A' Level, then applied to join Pye electrical factory. That was in 1972. I did a year's training making horseshoes, welding, and making transistor radios.

Peter Brown, born 1935

In The Old Days

Before television existed, old people went to the pub, the British Legion,

etc. I remember my grandmother, she used to sit outside her house with her red shawl round her shoulders and watch people go by, she would just sit. When I was young I never thought about being old, it never entered my head. Old people are looked after more than they used to be, they used to be left alone a lot, not helped as they are today. I feel looked after, but I often think about dying, it doesn't worry me. I've had a good life and, as long as I don't suffer, I don't care, I'm ready to go when the time comes.

Gladys Bateman, born 1909

Chesterton Hospital

Chesterton Geriatric Hospital is a former workhouse, when I arrived in 1973 it was run by a very progressive man who wasn't prepared to accept that old age meant that was it. He believed the conditions of old age could be treated and life maximised. There was goodwill in the hospital and the treatment was first-class. There was a spin-off from the workhouse days, there were long-stay people who were not necessarily very ill.

Des Cusack, born 1942

The Good Old Times

When I was young the old people then accepted charity with dignity. One I knew had been a cook-housekeeper, she was very dignified. I spent a lot of time with her, she taught me a lot of household skills. She was

Richard Carter (left) 'trying to be cool' on holiday in Scotland, 1972.

quiet and unassuming, a calm and constant character. It was a consistent and safe kind of life. Life isn't like that now.

Judy Fox, born 1955

Student Days

As a student I came across drugs, but I never felt the need to try any, I just didn't fancy it. I had a very good moral upbringing from my parents and now I don't need to know what it feels like. I've been drunk enough to know what it's like to be intoxicated. Now it's quite different anyway, the police are not down on cannabis nearly so much as they were.

Richard Carter, born 1955

Learning and Healing

I returned to Cambridge after my studies. I had trained as a physiotherapist. I found it strange, having a white coat on, I was a 'healing woman', and it was quite a powerful position. It was quite a different position from being in school. The college had been set up for students with visual problems who wanted to do physiotherapy, a 'blind career'. My mother had hopes I would marry a rich consultant. I found learning about the body was very fascinating. Failing my exams was very disappointing, my studies had been keeping me together. I came back to Cambridge and got a job at Ida Darwin Hospital. At the time (1979-80) unemployment was just under a million, I had gone to the job centre and the man there said to me, 'normal people

Village lads in the 1940s. Left: Stan Topham, right: Harry Tack.

can't get jobs, so a blind person like you won't have much hope.' I was so angry I was determined I would get a job, and I did. I got a job helping people with daytime activities, they had very difficult jobs, but I made two close friends, the sort of friends you have for life. When I was twenty-six I decided to go and do a degree. I realised I was in a dead-end position, I was eager to get on, and didn't want to wait for opportunities to arise through work. I went to Nottingham and did a degree in social policy. I got my degree aged twenty-nine.

Lynne Hester, born 1960

Aches and Pains

I don't like getting old, I don't like the aches and pains, or the idea of selling my bungalow. I'll hate not leaving it to my son to inherit, but when I go to hospitals and homes to speak to people, I think how lucky I am to be able to walk out of the door when they can't.

Dora Tack, born 1921

CHAPTER 6

Technology

In Memory of

Rifleman Arthur Albert Player

2nd Bn., Rifle Brigade
who died aged 20 on Tuesday, 23rd August 1916.

Rifleman Player was the son of Arthur William and Louisa
Player, of 10, Manbey Rd., The Grove, Stratford.

Remembered with honour
VERMELLES BRITISH CEMETERY.

THEIR NAME LIVETH
FOR EVERMORE

In the perpetual care of
the Commonwealth War Graves Commission

Certificate from the Commonwealth War Graves Commission's webpage. Kris Neilson tracked this document down while surfing the internet.

Other Jobs

We used to grow potatoes but not now, the soil is too light, and we couldn't get the workforce. It was labour-intensive work, long and arduous. Now you can do more with combine harvesters in one hour, than in a day in the days of horses and binders.

After the war I came straight back to Britain and I was demobilised and went back to farming. During the war I worked in the medical corps, and would have preferred to remain in some kind of medical work afterwards, but my father was tired and I felt it was my duty to take on the farm. In those days almost everyone in the village was a farmer or farm labourer, now you can count them on the fingers of one hand. People go into Wisbech, do factory work, and other jobs, and a lot of retired people have come in.

Norman Pentelow, born 1922

On The Farm

When I was a boy, I worked on the farm. Everything had to be done by hand: the hoeing of the corn, all the weeding was done by hand: the wild oats, they made us wild! Also binding the corn, and stacking it into shocks – we called that a shocking job! Our arms would always be sore because we had to carry the corn and it chafed, the corn had to be ripened in the sun after it was cut, and some of the fields were 300 yards long, so we had to carry the corn all that way. Sometimes we had to carry a heavy bag of potatoes over a plank crossing a dike, we were scared to fall in.

It was hot work and the only drink we had was cold tea, but some people used to drink the river water. We always took our food to the fens, we called it 'docky'. It's thought the name came from a farmer who caught a landworker eating on the job and said he was paid to work, not to eat, and so the farmer said he would 'dock'ee your pay' – hence docky time! Docky was a loaf of bread with pieces taken out, and margarine – or in our case always butter, because father had cows – and either a lump of cold pork or lump of cheese put with the bread, then this was wrapped in a cloth – sometimes a hessian sack (we called it a docky bag) – and we ate the docky with a penknife, called a shutknife. A good farm labourer always carried a shutknife, a piece of string and a shilling because it was said they'd always come in handy. You'd cut pieces off the docky with the knife. Once in a factory I was told off for eating my food on the shop floor because it was unhygienic. I laughed, because I recalled when we used to eat our docky on a muck-cart, a cart that had previously carried manure!

John Martin, born 1926

Housework Made Easier

I recall my first electric appliances, a little black Hoover, a little square-tub washing machine with a tiny tub and a wringer. This lasted a couple of years, then a Hoover representative came round and suggested a new machine. Then in the 1960s I had a Hoover automatic, it was out of this world. Then I had a Hotpoint, since then I've been a fiend for Hotpoint. Now I have a tumble-dryer, these aren't luxuries, if you go out to work they're necessities. If there's anything else new I'll have it, no doubt about that!

When I first went out to work in 1958, I had the barest necessities. I had to be very careful with my money, I had to increase my hours to supplement Tom's salary. This made it possible for me to buy various appliances. It's a circular thing, if you have mod cons, you have an easier life, if you have an easier life, you have less stress, more patience and time to do things.

Iris Crossley, born 1924

Arthur Player.

Pink and Blue

I went to work at Pye's in the woodcraft section which made wooden cabinets for radios. The Pye in St Andrews Road used to be the same one that was called Telecom, which was in Newmarket Road. Which is where I was first trained, you actually made wire baskets, and soldered the points where you'd wound the wire round the other one. I worked there for a while, and they had different rooms: one was a pink room, one was a blue room, and a yellow room, for different sorts of work you did. The blue room, all the girls in there wore a blue overall, or the other room was a pink overall, so they could tell if you were in the wrong room, if you went visiting somebody in the pink room, it stood out a mile because you wore a blue overall. The supervisors would know if you were chatting with someone you shouldn't have been chatting with.

Grace Robinson, born 1940

Surfing the Internet

I have surfed the internet, I did this to find out about my grandmother's brothers who died in the First World War. She had wanted to go and find her brothers' graves, but never did. I heard about a web site on the radio, and so I surfed the net and got a magical bit of paper, a certificate of information. It gives the grave reference number. My mother doesn't understand how I got the information.

Kris Neilson, born 1949

Shire Horses

We worked with shire horses. Once I took a horse to the blacksmith to be shoed; the horses would lean on the blacksmith for support, and the blacksmith didn't like it. He told me to talk to the horse to get him to move, he said I should tell him his mother was dead, but the horse took no notice! The horses were lovely gentle animals, they hardly ever kicked anyone. The boys would lead the horses for hoeing and the older men would walk behind guiding the hoe. I was one of the boys who led the horses. The boys would get very tired, and the men would reproach the boys for slacking. But later I realised that the boys had by far the hardest part of the task. The men would say 'run here boy, run there' – never use the boy's name. It was a hard life and the boys felt put upon by the men. But later the boys grew up into men who did the same thing to the next generation!

John Martin, born 1926

Factory Worker

The only thing we didn't do during the training at Pye was woodwork, but everyone had done that at school, and anyway, the days of the wooden radio cabinets were long over, everything was plastic by then. In 1973 I went into the factory, on a production line with fifty women, but I was still completely innocent. I then carried on, through the various areas of the factories. I listened to what people said, sometimes the language was quite blue. Things I'd never heard about before. In my spare time I was into ham radio, amateur radio. I lived, breathed, and slept radios.

The main production workforces were women, everything was hand-made, hand-crafted. We would put components into the printed circuit boards, cut them off to the right size, and assemble them into frames ready for soldering. We would also wire things up. I worked with radios, for the police, fire brigade, taxi drivers, walkie-talkies, I have a collection, which I have kept in the shed, my own private museum.

Now the things that are made are so complicated, you can't compare them with what we made then. Then you could understand everything, but now

A war office letter notifying Arthur Player's family of his death, 1916.

Richard Carter's police car, St Ives.

everything moves so fast, it's very difficult to keep up. Then if something didn't work you could get inside and mend it, now you throw it away, or send it to a specialist with good eyesight. Things got smaller but my fingers stayed the same size.

Peter Brown, born 1954

The Float Person

When you started up the lines in the factory they used to have somebody which they called a float. They used to work up the line, so you could go to the toilet and not stop the flow of the work. Say you had twenty positions in a job, you worked on one long bench, and you'd do your piece of work, and it would be passed on to the next person. If you wanted to go to the toilet, you'd call them and they'd come in and relieve you while you went to the toilet, or they'd start up at the beginning and work each one, so you could go off. If you needed to go an extra time, you could put your hand up and they'd come and relieve you. The float person had to know every stage of the job, so she got a little bit better pay, and it was up to you to try and work yourself to that position.

Grace Robinson, born 1940

Leaving the Land

I gave up farm working because it was such hard work, picking potatoes, stooping all the time in all weathers, and going in the dykes. I got such backache, sometimes I couldn't walk straight. We always got colds, and stuffed up from thrashing. There was a porter's job going at Shippea Hill Station, my wife didn't like it because it was shift work and she didn't want me to work shifts. But I went for it and got it. I think if I hadn't, if I'd stayed on the

91

land, I would have been crippled or dead. It happened to a lot of farmworkers I knew.

Harry Bye, Born 1917

Talking Computers

I now work for Cambridge City Council; so much is on computer. Because I can't see, I have a package on my computer called 'Jaws for Windows', it does everything via the spoken voice, it talks to me. It's the voice, the same as the one Professor Stephen Hawking, the disabled scientist, uses. So it's like spending the whole day with Professor Stephen Hawking, it's quite an experience.

Lynne Hester, born 1960

On the Buses

Philips was a good firm, one of the best to work for. They came from as far as King's Lynn, Peterborough, Downham Market, Haverhill, Bury St Edmunds, Royston, St Neots, Bedford, all that way to work there. There were buses which would pick people up from various locations, when I first got picked up it was a double-decker; it hadn't got doors on it, just a metal bar in the middle, and you used to put a blanket up the door to keep warm. It was frightening to be on top, because you'd go round Twenty Pence Road on these buses, with the thin, twisting roads, it wasn't so funny. You went through Cottenham, Wilburton, to Haddenham, if it was icy it was quite a nightmare. I remember once when there were snowdrifts each side and the driver got us through.

Grace Robinson, born 1940

Ironmongery

Someone came in to our hardware shop to buy a bucket of the type people used to use as a toilet, now they use it for coal. He came back and said it had holes in it. It used to be made to be water tight, but now it's used for coal, so it's not sealed so well as it was then. But he obviously still wanted to use it as a toilet bucket! We still sell the old galvanised baths. Now they're mainly used for dogs, but one old lady bought one a few weeks ago and was obviously still using it as intended. Our best-selling item is the mousetrap. That's changed too. Many people nowadays don't want to kill the mice, so we have to ask whether they want a type of mousetrap that will kill the mice or humane ones.

I believe families stay together less now because of the fire, in the old days if you had a fire and no central heating, children wouldn't go to their bedrooms, everyone would congregate where the fire was, to keep warm. Now with central heating, the family distributes itself around the house. I wish it weren't so because I miss them. I love it when we all sit together and watch a TV programme as a family.

Diana Philipott, born 1951

Johnson's shop front today.

Computing In Schools

Our school is going on line with sixty terminals, going on the Internet, you've got to keep up with technology, but you can take out the social engagement, the fact that you're human, young people don't realise that.

Marc Thornley, born 1967

Workers Playtime

You found you could talk and laugh and joke; in the old factory you never had radios. But they used to have Workers' Playtime come on through the speaker system; somebody upstairs would be putting records on, or they'd put the radio on, in the new factory they put headphones with the radio with six stations on every bench, so you'd have your headphones on, and put them to whatever station you wanted. So you had Radio 1, Radio Cambridgeshire, Hereward, or whatever, but at half past one in the afternoons when it used to come to the story time, you could always tell, it was dead quiet, and then in the mornings at eleven o'clock you used to have a sob story told on one of the stations, and you'd see tears coming down people's eyes, so you knew what they were listening to. It was fun, it was the best years of my working life.

Grace Robinson, born 1940

Understanding Technology

The technology is a tool, it has a use. But the compulsion to keep up with all the latest technology makes me feel vulnerable, if we don't do it, someone

Godmanchester, 1936.

else will. In my computer business you have to find an angle that sells, we excel in the video conferencing area – e.g. for the NHS. Their understanding of technology in the NHS is very poor, so we have to make the software very simple. It is a growing area, the computer business is a cottage industry; people in bedrooms doing important work, not specific to any area, even though Cambridge is ostensibly the centre, we can link to California, Boston, it's a light industry, service-related. I enjoy it now because my partners and I are running our own business.

Colin Warlow, born 1960

Three-Day Week

I worked at the factory when there was a three-day week (in 1972), and we went into power cuts, and they brought in their own generators. We used to work until nine o'clock at night, they used to supply us with a hot meal, because it was three days' working, and three days off. We were making parts for the soldiers in Ireland, on their backpacks, where they put the batteries in, that was their two-way radio systems. Just as I got home my electricity would go off, so I went home to darkness! People all worked to keep it going, and if we worked over our hours we used to get extra pay for that.

Grace Robinson, born 1940

CHAPTER 7
Lifestyle

Iris Crossley, March 1945.

The Chowns' Golden Wedding cake, created by Stanley Chown.

Difficult Summer

We didn't have a fridge, that was okay in the winter but very difficult in the summer. I recall going to parties at other children's houses and thinking how palatial they were. Having no father was normal though, it was our family unit, and what I was used to.

Lynne Hester, born 1960

Unaccompanied Minor

I had a friend from Spain who went to the same school as me, Newnham Croft in Cambridge. There are lots of children there from all over the world. My friend went back to Spain and when she left, she asked me to come and visit her in Spain. Then she would phone me and she kept asking me to come and visit her. I started badgering my mum, but she was afraid for me to go, she was afraid the plane might crash, or something else might happen. I wasn't frightened, I didn't think it would happen because the chances of a crash are very low, and anyway if there was a crash, I would probably die very quickly. Then my stepfather said to my mother, 'why don't you let her go, there's no harm, it's safer for her to go in a plane to Spain because she's always with an adult, than it is for her to go to school by herself.' So I went as an 'unaccompanied minor', that means, unaccompanied by a parent, but a stewardess came and took me on the plane, and another boy who was on his own as well. He'd done the journey before, and he told me what to expect from the flight while we were waiting.

The thing I remember most about it is looking out and seeing that we were above the clouds, the fluffy white clouds, and the loud noise of the engine all through the flight. My friend lives in Madrid, it's a beautiful city with gardens and lots of flowers. Sometimes we walked through the city, but mostly we drove, to places like McDonalds!

Rachel Kanev, born 1989

A Christmas Meal

Towards the end of the war, we knew things were moving. At Christmas 1944, I had got some food smuggled through into the jungle where we were prisoners of war. I got some medicine bottles from the dispensary, filled them with coloured water and put the names of vintage wines on, as a joke. For our Christmas dinner I cooked little fish, and I minced rice and moulded it into shapes. After the war, I was given an award for my efforts.

Stanley Chown, born 1911

Milk Churns

The milk was in churns and they used to put ladles into it to measure it and pour it into the jugs: You would go to the cart, and they would dip the ladles with the long handles into the churns to bring out a half pint or a pint, and you would put it straight into your jug. There were no fridges then, but we had meat safes with a mesh at the front which you kept in the coldest place in the house. We used cumulators to run the radios instead of batteries: there was battery acid in them and if you touched it and tasted it, it tasted nasty.

Grace Robinson, born 1940

No Meat

When I was a child, meals were often quite frugal. My mother was famous for her meatless stews, she could buy on credit and run up a tab. I recall my dad coming home on a Friday at 4.30 with his pay packet and then we'd dash madly to the market to get food before they closed down. It was mostly meat and vegetables and potatoes. My dad liked curry, having served in India. But he wasn't allowed to have that because mother couldn't stand the smell. We always had a Sunday roast. I remember being sent out for the meat and told not to spend more than 7s 6d.

Judy Fox, born 1955

Private Parties

Cooking in the university was very interesting, there were lots of private lunches and dinners: crèmes brûlées were popular. I put the college coat of arms at each place on the table.

I would often stay on in the college kitchen to perfect a creation instead of going home to my wife. I had a particular way of decorating cakes. When I first went to work at the

One of Stanley Chown's menus, signed by Prince Charles.

college the students were mostly hunting and shooting types; sons and grandsons of former students, but then they changed, there were more grammar school types.

Once I was asked to serve 1,500-1,800 people. I said I could do it in half an hour, they doubted this but I did it in twenty-five minutes. I met Prince Charles and other royalty. I have an MBE.

Stanley Chown, born 1911

Gardening

Nowadays, most people think of their gardens for recreation. When I was a child, most people grew vegetables, but by the 1970s people wanted their gardens for pleasure, barbecues were coming in, and people wanted nice big lawn and patios.

Judy Fox, born 1955

Crusty Bread

The village shop was where you could get split peas and sugar was weighed and put into blue bags, butter and lard was patted and put into grease-proof paper. Cheese was round and in a muslin cloth, the bread was locally baked – nice and crusty, we used to pick the crust off before we got home. Plums we used to pick, and local apples – sometimes we used to scrump those! People were very friendly. The summers were hot and we could go to bed and leave our doors and windows wide-open, never any fear of anyone walking in that shouldn't.

Grace Robinson, born 1940

Mondays

We had leftovers on Monday – washday – and Bubble and Squeak. On Tuesday we had rissoles, and the leftovers went into the stewpot. We also had milk slop, which was vile stuff, disgusting! I didn't feel deprived at the time, we were well off compared with some people. I can recall people who were even worse off than I was, an old neighbour who used to get the pig potatoes, they were small potatoes (now so fashionable) which then were usually reserved for the pigs.
But she was well off compared with the lady down the road who had no family and literally relied on everyone else feeding her. We never threw anything away, even leftover gravy would be saved for her and taken over in a screw top jar. I would be sent over with it, she lived totally on other people's leftovers. But it was quite normal then, there were a lot of people who had no income. Even now I sometimes feel guilty, I've become more throw-away, and throw leftover food in the bin, but I still sometimes take leftovers to an elderly lady who lives three doors away.

Judy Fox, born 1955

Rationing

We lived in Needingworth Road in St Ives where I grew up and stayed there until I was married at twenty-four. We were wartime children; my mother cooked a stew in a pot, the pot went the rounds of the neighbours. There was rationing, if we were lucky we had an egg on Sunday morning, and might have a rabbit. We didn't have the selection we have today, but we were healthier, more vegetables. One of my best dishes now is Yorkshire pudding, and I try to cook three courses.

Lillian Melton, born 1932

Richard Carter and wife, Linda, on their wedding day, 27 March 1995.

Interior of the Rex Cinema, Ely, now a Boots store.

Cannibals

There's a myth that gypsies steal children and eat them. Once some hippies tried to sell my wife some children, to eat. They thought we were cannibals and murderers. The press play a big part in misrepresenting us.

Peter Mercer, born 1935

Redundant

I left when the job I was doing became redundant, it went to another place, and double days stopped. So instead of being £200 a week, which I was on then, in 1990, it went down to about £160. I'd been there twenty years in that one factory, so I took redundancy and went to agency work. The workforce started scaling down when I actually took redundancy, they weren't putting new staff on, just taking contract workers on, so then they could say, 'right, the job's not there any more, you just go and find another job'.

They could cut the workforce down, because you ran the section on a fraction of what you had before. When it first took off you had about fifty or sixty people in that area; I should think it runs on about fifteen or twenty now at the most. Before you did hand soldering, where then the machine could do it.

Grace Robinson, born 1940

Cookery bygones

I remember puddings made with suet, spotted dick, but now people go in for ready-made food, in a microwave, now I mostly cook casseroles. In my youth a chicken was something special, now it's commonplace. Food from World War Two was dried egg etc. A friend of mine, her daughter was at school doing cookery and the teacher told her to buy pastry from the supermarket.

Dorothy Grubb, born 1908

Microphone

Once I was on a stage giving a performance when the microphone packed up. So I walked to the front of the stage and spoke without it and everyone could still hear. Sir Henry Irving's granddaughter happened to be in the audience, and she congratulated me on my audibility. I told her I had been influenced by her grandfather, who was a famous nineteenth-century actor-manager, and who had always insisted on the importance of being heard at the back of a theatre. Then she and I started to exchange correspondence. I collect theatre memorabilia and I had some copies of letters concerning her family, which I sent to her. She sent me a book.

Eric Nicholson, born 1925

Puddings

When I left the Army, I got a job in a school, as a cook. I cooked for two schools: fish and chips, roast beef, stews, steamed puddings, spotted dick, treacle pudding, custard. I made it all from scratch.

Gladys Bateman, born 1909

Sunday Treats

It was a treat to go over to Christ's Pieces and watch the band play, sometimes we used to go and sit on Parker's Piece to Hobb's Pavilion and watch the cricket. Another treat was to walk up to the Rosemary pub and sit outside with a packet of crisps and a glass of lemonade. We used to go to Sunday school and church – Baptist church – every Sunday, and if you were regular with the Bible class you used to get a trip to Clayhithe up the river. We used to get on the boat near the Victoria Bridge, take a packed lunch, and sit on the bridge near the hotel at Clayhithe and have our lunch there as a treat. Going through the lock was quite an experience – seeing all that water in front of you, and it was low at the back, frightening. We used to go up in the boat, and then have to wait for the man to come and wind the lock, and then water would level up, you would go up as the water came down, it was a treat we looked forward to because it was the only time you ever went out of town, because trips to the seaside were never on, we never had the money. I loved being on the water, it was a way of transport we'd never known before, and it was something you only did once a year for so long.

Grace Robinson, born 1940

Meal Times

I think going out for a meal is special, because we don't do it very often. Now people have more money and give each other more expensive things. But

Geoffrey Allgood's brother's barrel-engine, Kneesworth, 1930s.

health is important, money doesn't make you happy. When I go shopping I buy fruit and vegetables, sausages, the children love those, a joint, fish, bacon, egg, sausage rolls, fish fingers, beef burgers, and pizza for when the children have friends over. It's cheaper to buy fresh food. We rarely all eat together. I eat with the children, and my husband eats later. On Sunday mornings we go to church, and we have a snack at lunchtime and a big roast dinner at teatime.

Louella Prince, born 1961

Being Poor

When I grew up we had nothing, and yet we had everything. Back then we were ignorant, we were happy with nothing, but now I wouldn't be happy in a freezing cold house, with stone floors, sacks on the floor, and a hole in the ground for a toilet. But we didn't know anything then, now life is easier and we expect more.

Geoffrey Allgood, born 1913

Yuletide

When I was a kid, we made presents for people, it would be a nice thing to work for. I remember a silk-screen I made for my mother, based on Rilke's poem, 'The Sea it Cleansed me with its Noise', I was about thirteen, and a teacher at school helped me with it.

Molly Andrews, born 1959

102

Making Your Own Clothes

My mother used to do dressmaking, so people would help her out with food. My father and brother both died. So we had to live off my mother's dressmaking. When we moved my mother carried on with her job. When she was sixty she got her old age pension and thought she had the world, she had her independence. That was in the 1920s.

Meg Tuck, born 1902

Spotted Dick

Everything was rationed, so food was basic, steak and kidney puddings, bacon and onion rolls, spotted dicks, steamed puddings, and fruit which you picked like blackberries for blackberry and apple pie, also you had jam tarts, mince pies; you were well fed, you were never hungry, and at Xmas I remember you'd bought the bread and you'd dip it in a bucket of water and put it back in the oven to freshen it up. At Xmas you had mince pies, an orange, a few nuts in a bag, and one present for each of us, and it was a luxury to have a chicken, we looked forward to it. Sundays we had basically jelly and ice cream.

Grace Robinson, born 1940

Manea, 1930.

Kiddle's furniture and carpet shop, one of St Ives' oldest (100 years plus) and best known shops, closed in the late 1980s.

Spending

I went to work for the local council and earned £2.15 a week. I gave my mother £2 and had the rest to spend. I used to go to the cinema, I watched anything and everything. The worst times were when we had real financial problems, my son had had a nice lifestyle when I was still married to his father. But my present husband couldn't afford to buy him new shoes, so he insisted we didn't go out or spend any money until we had £1,000 behind us. He was a farm worker, and earned £44 a week.

Billie Bridgement, born 1935

On The Bread Line

Most of the income when I was little came from Social Security, our house was very cold, the windows were frozen on the inside. I would be sent to other people's houses, with my old clothes we thought people might buy. Many people did buy them. Even now, the people with the lowest incomes are often the ones who worry most about their children being different and having poor clothes, whereas I would go into Oxfam to buy clothes and not bat an eyelid. We lived on fish-paste and jam sandwiches. Christmas and birthdays were really stressful times.

Lynne Hester, born 1960

Joint Bank Account

My wife Linda is the driving force. She takes care of the finances for us. She deals with bills and the mortgage. I don't even know what the mortgage is. She enjoys dealing with accounting, whereas I don't. We have no financial secrets, we have a joint bank account. It's not my money or her money but 'our' money. My father dealt with the finances for my parents, until he had his stroke, then my mother dealt with it.

Steve Hill, born 1957

Navy Knickers

We were always clean and well-dressed, at Easter you used to get a new dress. Then your best dress that was could go for playing or for schooling, and the other clothes went for playing; you stepped your clothes down. Father used to used to sole our shoes when they needed mending, he'd put studs all round the bottoms and the heels, and we used to slide and make sparks come out the bottom, we had some fun. We used to slide down the ice in the spinney, down the hill, now you look at it and think, the danger you were in; we'd slide on a sledge and on our backside, we wore many a knicker bottom out! We used to have those old big navy knickers, with the elastic round the waist and the legs, you used to have to roll them up and make them look smaller, and your handkerchief was kept up your knicker leg. We used to have to wear liberty bodices that had rubber buttons and you could button a skirt onto it. Then we had kilt-like skirts that you could button on. Mother was one for knitting white twin-sets with roses round, she was good at Fair-Isle, later in life she was good at Arran knitting, so we were never short of good clothes.

Grace Robinson, born 1940

Shopping

I often dream about shopping; about craft shops. I look forward to it. Not doing the food shopping. If I have money, I have to spend it. I could spend £300-400 in a couple of days. I bought myself a coat, we buy toys, things for the computer, my husband buys photographic equipment. I buy clothes, mostly coats. I have forty or fifty different coats which hang in the wardrobe, all the same style, isn't that what people addicted to shopping do? I'll feel a real excitement if I know I'm going shopping the next day, sometimes I can't sleep, I love looking. On a good day I might buy five to six items of clothing. My husband is brilliant, and goes with me. He buys a magazine, and then trails around behind me reading and selecting things for me to try on. It's brilliant to have a man who loves shopping, but I do feel guilty, partly because other members of my family don't have the kind of money I have, often if I have bought something I won't tell them.

Linda Hill, born 1961

Single Parents

The value of money has changed a lot since I was little. My mum didn't get housing benefit, so in that way I'm better off than she was. They don't give single parents enough to live on now. Jobs are very hard to come by and fathers don't pay.

Donna Mawby, born 1967

Agreements

I remember arguments for hours over a few pennies on the cost of the grain, when the deal was done, they shook hands and that was a binding deal, nothing in writing, but no going back on it either.

Terry Huggins, born 1934

Juggling The Finances

I have a lot of financial difficulties, especially because I smoke it's a struggle to make ends meet and to juggle financial needs. Sometimes you have to decide – do you pay the bills or go out, not to the pub or anything, but just to see a friend. I'm in a benefits trap and find it difficult.

Sally Scott, born 1965

Like Winning The Lottery

I was quite happy with the redundancy payout that I got, although afterwards I did regret leaving, because once you've been inside Phillips, you've got used to that work, you've got used to the way they think, and it was an easy way of life.

I got £11,000 redundancy for doing twenty years – three month's severance pay, and the rest was redundancy. I went out and bought furniture for my home, a three-piece suite which I'd never had before, I used to have easy chairs, I bought a new fridge-freezer, I bought my motorbike, and got everything shipshape, as I wanted it. I felt secure for the first time in my life, my marriage broke up and when I moved I replaced everything. So there wasn't a lot of my previous home left, so all I've got together is me, my new partner can't say it's your old life, it's all my new life. I spent all the money, and I enjoyed doing it.

It was nice to go out and know that you'd got the cash to be able to buy a three-piece, and a fridge-freezer, you weren't thinking, 'well, I've got to get it out of a club, or I've got to get a second-hand one'. It was nice to know it was new, and it was also *my* money, so I could go out and choose *my* choice. It wasn't anybody else's choice, it was mine, completely mine, it was like winning a small amount on the lottery, you go out and spend all you want, I had great fun in doing it.

Grace Robinson, born 1940

Trust

Once when I was a girl I went out for a walk with some boys and got back late and had to ring the bell, I told the woman I worked for that I had had a puncture. The old lady didn't trust me, so I let my front tyre down and had to pump it up again later. Girls didn't get into trouble then as they do now, I would beware of life now.

I wasn't very keen on the fierce old lady though, I got 3s 6d a week, and gave my mother 5s a month for washing. We didn't go out much except when my friends and I went for walks. We met some boys in Huntingdon, they offered us girls cigarettes, mine made me sick and I've never smoked since.

Emily Upchurch, born 1915

All Alone

I am pretty solitary, I prefer to spend a lot of time alone. I read, paint my models, I read fantasy science fiction, adventures, also non-fiction such as encyclopaedias. I like to pick one up, choose and read a page at random and to look at what's at the bottom as alternative references and to look at that. Our family has a computer. It's a pretty old one, it is used for word-processing and school work, no games. We're getting a better one.

Andrew Dunkley, born 1985

What Can We Do?

I had been lucky as a teenager, had loads of friends and we were the first in the village to have a telephone, so I could ring people and gossip. I had a good friend, Paul, who passed his driving test early on, and used to take me wherever I wanted to go, which was

lovely. We were limited in our entertainment, in the village we had a pub, a post box, and a telephone box. There had been a shop but it closed, there was a bus into Oundle once a week, and into Peterborough nearly every day, but you'd have to come home about 3 p.m., so we made our own entertainment, and stayed overnight with each other. But most of my time was taken up with Donny Osmond, he was my hero.

Linda Hill, born 1961

Saving

My brother's generation is more free, they go out more than I did. They travel on trains, to Peterborough and Cambridge. My friends and I went to other people's houses, more than meeting outside. I also spent a lot of time helping in the shop, but I had a good childhood. I got a lot of things I wanted. I had to save up a lot, through pocket money, Christmas and birthday presents. I saved for a stereo, and computer. My first computer gave me a lot of enjoyment, and I learned a lot.

Gavin Philpott, born 1980

Social Life

When we lived in Holme Fen we didn't have a social life, only on Saturday night. My father would take my mum to her mother, he'd go to the pub for a few drinks, then he'd go and see his mother. Meanwhile we children would go to the pictures at Ramsey in the 9d

Raymond Law in his portering days at Trinity College, 1983.

seats and buy an ice cream. A woman in the pub would make sandwiches for us children, then we'd go home.

Terry Huggins, born 1934

Royal Visit

I used to be very active in SIMADS – the St Ives Music and Amateur Dramatic Society. I was a leading light, singing, acting, doing costumes. I won an award for twenty-five years of service, and was presented to the Queen Mother. When I went to Buckingham Palace, I was warned not to mention St Ives to her because of Oliver Cromwell, so when she asked me where we came from I said, 'near

Huntingdon', she said, 'you mean St Ives, don't you? – I bet you were told not to say that to me!'

Lillian Melton, born 1932

Singing

When I was young we had a village hall and dances, but there aren't so many today. There was a tennis club and an outside bowls rink, a men's institute, we played billiards and snooker. Now I'm in a choir, we sing in Peterborough Cathedral, and at King's College Cambridge. It's the great occasion of the week to sing in the choir.

Norman Pentelow, born 1922

Snakes and Rats

I became a chef as quite a young man, and cooked at Pembroke College in Cambridge. At the start of the Second World War, I volunteered for hospital cooking and was eventually sent to the Far East. We went on a ship, heading for Singapore, to drop behind Japanese lines. But when we reached Singapore, our side was disorganised, our guns were round the wrong way, and everything degenerated into chaos. After a time we ran out of ammunition, and also water and other provisions, and we were surrounded by the Japanese. At 4 p.m. the ceasefire order went out, and we were captured. I was assigned to a hospital, cooking for the patients and personnel, about 1,800 to 2,000 people. I was ordered to take over the hospital's main cookhouse on the hill. It wasn't bad being a prisoner there. Then word came that a group were going to an island. All my friends were going, so I asked to go too. But I soon realised this was quite a different situation: We were put in cattle trucks, I got malaria, others had dysentery, and the trucks stank. We embarked on a forced march, always marching at night. Many of the men dropped out along the way – they were despatched by Japanese machine guns. We arrived at the camp, then cholera came, many more died. This was the Railway of Death, the Burma Railroad. I was put in charge of cooking again, and this saved my life, I couldn't have stood up to working on the railway. All the people were treated so badly – including their own; if any of their own men fell ill with malaria, they would just tie a piece of bamboo round his waist and drag him along until he died. But the extraordinary thing was that the Japanese, brutal though they were to their captives and their own people, couldn't kill a chicken – they asked me to do it for them! I managed to get hold of two chickens, and sneaked one away which I shared with my mates – one person said it was the best meal he ever had. But they didn't live long to remember it. I became famous for my snake and rat stew: It sounds disgusting, but it was all goodness, nutrition that would help keep people alive. In the jungle there was very little else to eat, mainly just rice, sometimes some eggs. I did what I could to help keep the sick prisoners alive.

Stanley Chown, born 1911

Sundays

When we were young, we made our own fun, at weekends we would go up to Hunstanton and play on the beach, we had a beach hut there, as did other trades people, and their children would play there too. We would all meet up, I enjoyed that; every Sunday was the same, tomato soup and a tin of corned beef. We had to queue for ages on the road to get up to there, people say you queue now, but people did then and nobody really complained. Things haven't changed that much but now we don't have the patience for them. We had a Zephyr car, with a big boot and a van for deliveries in the Fens, we used to play in the back because it was like a big room. One day it broke down

Stanley Chown, aged eighty-eight.

and never came back, it was pushed into a field and used by a farmer as a shed.

Diana Philipott, born 1951

Trains

I started travelling: The first time I went with some friends by train around Europe – Germany, Austria, Switzerland, Italy, Yugoslavia, Romania. Once we went to sleep and woke up in an oil field in southern Romania. It was fun because I was interested in steam trains, one time we were desperate for a cup of tea on the train and my friend disappeared with his ex-Army gas-mask case, three tin mugs, and a gas stove. He came back with three steaming mugs of tea, which he'd brewed up in the washroom on the train. It wasn't allowed, but he'd done it anyway. On my last trip to Iraq we stopped off in Jordan. I was offered a job there, later I went there on secondment from my company. Jackie, the woman who became my wife, was one of the secretaries in the office.

Peter Brown, born 1954

Never To Old To Fly

After my husband died I started travelling. I had never flown, and never wanted to, but my family had booked a trip to Lanzarote and I decided I'd like to go. I was eighty and I have now been there three times. I've also been to Austria and Tenerife, they were lovely, and I regret that I'd denied my late husband going because I wouldn't fly.

I looked out of the window of the plane and was so interested that I wasn't afraid. A niece of mine went to Spain and built a villa and invited me to go there to live in a granny flat, but I refused.

Meg Tuck, born 1902

Teenage Travel

As a young child I did more than other children, but as a teenager I remembered how vulnerable I was. I became panicked and remembered journeys equalled panic. I left school and was in London doing a course, going on the tube was absolutely terrifying, it wasn't to do with my lack of sight, it was all in my head. I was absolutely terrified. My mother died when I was eighteen. I had to make a journey home, that's when I realised the fear was all in my head.

Lynne Hester, born 1960

Holiday Romance

Once I was on holiday with my parents in Llandudno and a chap came up and asked me to dance, and then asked me to go on somewhere else afterwards. I asked him how old he was and he said he was twenty-four, I asked him how old he thought I was. He thought I was about nineteen or twenty, I said 'I'm twelve, do you still want to take me?' and he literally leapt back like a Harrier Jump Jet with a look of shock and horror and was gone!

Linda Hill, born 1961

Mill Road, Cambridge, 1978.

Early Morning Starts

When I was a boy I was in the Wolf patrol. Once, I went to the Lake District, it took a day to get there. We'd leave at 4 in the morning and arrive at 8 p.m. A friend used to go from Peterborough to Scotch Corner and that took a day, and it was another day to Penrith. I took my young lad more recently and we got there in three hours.

Brian Pearce, born 1949

Airforce Travel

During the war, I was in the RAF and also in the Army. I wanted to join the aircrew and wanted to bomb Germany. I got in the Airforce, lasted eight months, but then I was sent for exams and was rejected because I failed them. Also although there were huge losses, there weren't as many as expected, so they didn't want all the volunteers to go. Some of those who'd been on operations over Germany were grounded, because they weren't needed.

John Martin, born 1926

Donkeys

When I was a child, we always had a holiday, we went to Skegness every year for several years. We had good fun, riding donkeys and going on the beach. Once an amusement park opposite our hotel burned down and we slept through it. I never heard a thing. Now my family and I like caravans, and going skiing and holidays abroad. It's easy to go across on the ferry to France. We had a holiday in Canada.

Brian Abblitt, born 1948

African Experience

I've lived in Zambia for a year, Kenya, Ethiopia, Sudan, Egypt, most of north east Africa. The 1970s were a time of opportunity, I did a study of the insurance industry and Kenneth Kaunda announced they would nationalise, so I was thrown into negotiation on behalf of the Zambian Government. I had to hold the fort on behalf of our Government and wrote a bit of the budget speech which the President delivered in Parliament. Something you don't get aged twenty-three/twenty-four at home! They needed help, you were judged for what you were and what you could do.

Bill Wicksteed, born 1945

Bus Service

When I was young, there were no buses in March, few cars, and there was a weekly carrier's cart, but mostly we used shanks's pony – in other words, we walked. My husband and I had no car until we were in our forties. In later years public transport did improve but now many areas are far more poorly served than they were pre-Beeching in the 1960s. Some have no regular bus services, and if there's ever any hope of improving traffic on the roads, this huge problem of dealing with rural transport will have to be grappled with.

Joan Mulgrew, born 1920

A recent picture of Joan Mulgrew.

CHAPTER 8
Living and dying

Paul Crossley and
his parents, 1968.

Coping with Death

I've started to watch people of my generation die, gradually, people of my age and in my family. Death is no longer a strange occurrence – it is like a bus that comes along, and stops every once in a while now. It is a more frequent visitor, and part of the mystery of death is no longer alive to me. Death is also about the closing down of chances and opportunities. I'm not a person who believes in the spiritual life, I don't have religious beliefs. So I believe that we must strive together to create the best society we can, but also respect and tolerate each other and strive to make sure that we're able to achieve the best that we can for each other.

I saw my father after he died and I did not see peace on his face, I saw a greyness, it was a face of stone really, and I didn't feel this was a man at peace, I didn't feel that he had reached his full term. And so I didn't feel personally that there was this comfort in death, this release in death. I saw something different.

Paul Crossley, born 1950

Back into Fashion

We run a traditional hardware shop that's stood on the site for well over 100 years.

My mother never helped in the shop, in the latter part of my grandmother's life she was ill, and my mother spent a lot of time looking after her and going to the hospital to see her. She died but my grandfather lived on. He was a chemist, from 1915. He worked until the NHS came in, then bought a chemist's shop. He would sell whisky and wine as well as medicines. He used to make up his own cough mixture for children, and it made your throat feel lovely.

Diana Philipott, born 1951

Losing My Baby

I haven't been happy recently, I lost my baby and have had a difficult relationship with the father. I have changed completely. I didn't know what life was about until I had lost the baby, it has changed what's important in life. I have never had a love like that either, before I saw the baby. If you have lost the thing you loved the most it is difficult to be the same, I don't see things as important and I don't value things as much now because in comparison to the baby they don't hold as much value.

Dominique Elliott, born 1973

Family Relationship

My brother and mother took my father to Disneyland in America, two wheelchairs. Later we entered my mother for a 'Mum of the Year' contest and she won. They sent a Rolls Royce to the house to pick her up. A week later dad died, it was as if he'd done it all, he'd had a stroke ten years previously, and he'd had enough.

Brian Pearce, born 1949

Sixteen-year-old Iris Crossley with permed hair in the early 1940s.

Skin Blemish

Milk was delivered in a pony and trap, some on a tradesbike. My father used to cycle and deliver various products. I had a skin blemish, psoriasis, on my knees and arms, it was very unusual in those days, and I grew up feeling inferior. It made my school life a misery. After I came to Cambridge it was diagnosed and was successfully treated at Addenbrooke's Hospital.

Iris Crossley, born 1924

Keeping Fit

I do my best to keep fit, once I was fat, it crippled my life and prevented me getting girlfriends. I hope the future will be good, because I'll inherit quite a bit from my dad and set myself up as a DJ. Hopefully we'll be able to live on the Moon or Mars, then we could equal the population out, start life somewhere else and try to not to pollute it.

John Booth, born 1983

Suicide

BSE has ruined many farmers, some commit suicide. I knew one farmer who got so uptight that he put a gun in his mouth and pulled the trigger, it got on top of him, the financial pressure. It's getting worse, good hard-working men working seven days a week and can't make ends meet, there's so much red tape, rules about wind-speed, and spraying, disposing of empty containers, etc.

Terry Huggins, born 1934

Cancer

I had bowel cancer and had to have chemotherapy. My health seems all right now. I have to have a CT scan in three weeks, but I feel well. As far as I know they cut it out. I had symptoms before I went to the doctor, intermittent bleeding. The diagnosis was a terrific shock, I went into hospital quite quickly and the operation was very straightforward, but the chemotherapy was awful. I'm only now beginning to come to terms with the emotional side of it, the horrendous side effects. I think if the cancer came back, I wouldn't be able to go through the chemotherapy again. But maybe, if that did happen, I would change my mind.

Sally Trepte, born 1950

Child Birth

I live in Isleham and go to school in Soham. I'm the oldest of three, I've got a younger sister, Sarah, and a younger brother, Christopher. In between there was another brother who died. He died because something went wrong during the birth, his heart stopped, they had to do a Caesarean, but he died after seven days. I was very little, but remember giving him a teddy bear, and I use that to remember him. I wasn't bothered at the time, but now I know that it troubled my parents tremendously. I felt it was my first brother, he looked so sweet, I wanted to do something. I was upset later, but can't say what I felt at the time. It has given the family a broader view on things and how they can affect us. It's now easier to accept things, because we know there's always something worse that can happen.

Andrew Dunkley, born 1985

Birth of Granddaughter

Because both my children were born by Caesarean, I'd never witnessed a normal birth. Seeing my granddaughter Alanah-Maire being born was the most fantastic thing I'd ever experienced, it was lovely becoming a grandmother. When Jayne was giving birth I was pushing with her. I've got a wonderful bond with my granddaughter now. When Jayne was rebelling and running away, I hated her, she was punishing me for getting rid of her dad. He could do no wrong, he'd indoctrinated her during the ten months we didn't see each other, after that I remarried and got custody of Jayne.

Sandra Wells, born 1955

Terrible Accident

My wife was driving a moped when a lorry came out of a turning and stopped in front of her, she ran into it and was thrown across the road. She sustained head injuries, broken limbs, ribs, pelvis, a punctured lung, and ten days later she had a complete stroke, which took away her speech and left her paralysed on one side. The doctors broke both of her arms to try to get them going. She suffered terribly, I don't know how she coped. She's quite right in the head despite her injuries, I taught her to write and say a few words. I used rhyming slang to teach her.

The hardest part of being a carer is not being able to do what you want, go where you want. There's respite care but she doesn't want to go into the places, sometimes I feel trapped, but while she's alive she's a companion to me. I can talk to her even though she can't answer me. Our marital life has gone for a burton, before her accident we weren't active every night but we didn't do too bad. She still wanted to, but every time I put my arms around her she started to shout with pain, so I stopped. I must have the record for 'non-sex'. It was very hard to bear at first, but now I'm used to it.

Raymond Law, born 1938

No Ambulances

There were no ambulances in those days, so I was taken to hospital in an ordinary car. I didn't care about losing the baby, I accepted having no

Raymond Law's wife is pictured outside 4 Portugal Street, Trinity Lodging House, Cambridge, 1980.

children, it didn't worry me because I had the cat; animals were my pets, I loved them. If I had the choice I would have loved to go into working with animals, but the war came and I went to work for the Red Cross.

Meg Tuck, born 1902

Sufferers

We were rarely ill as children, when the NHS was set up we thought everything would be fine, but I didn't need it. I remember people who went to Papworth, the TB sufferers. People thought it came from milk, but they used to drink milk straight from the cow.

Geoffrey Allgood, born 1913

Losing My Mother

The worst thing that ever happened to me was when my mother died. Then I had to look after my father, he was nearly eighty when he died. They were such good parents. My mother died at fifty-five of cancer, I was in my teens.

Gladys Bateman, born 1909

Left Alone

I'm widowed. We were two become one, and half the partnership went. It's a strange experience to be left as one. Some of my identity has gone, I loved being introduced as her husband.

I've had real problems with my identity, I thought I used to share the shopping in the supermarket, now I realise I was just holding the trolley. Someone said I would never be happy again, but I feel that's wrong. You can be happy in a different way, it's taken me two to three years to get to that point. Thirty years of marriage I can't replicate.

One is an odd number, so there's awkwardness about being single. Happiness now is different, achieving retirement, doing my open university course, meeting people who never knew me as part of a couple, but in my own right, they accept me as I am. A different 'me' is emerging. My wife's death was from cancer; there were five

weeks between diagnosis and her death. I was fortunate to have tremendous friends who helped me. I think I wouldn't like to have another relationship with a woman, but you should never say 'never'.

Des Cusack, born 1942

Unpleasant Death

My father has just died, I feel alone. I have one brother. The person I used to ask for advice has gone. I'm in the early part of middle age, I feel very alone, we were very close. It was a great tragedy to find out he was terminally ill. I found it hard to comprehend.

To know he couldn't think about the end of next week, or even tomorrow. I couldn't understand how I could live like that. My father didn't find it hard, he just said what was hard was the vacuum that it caused. I found that more difficult than dealing with my own death. He didn't die a very pleasant death, he died of stomach cancer. He was more worried about my stepmother than for his own children. Death to him was just another chapter, he was not scared of dying at all. He died at home, I wasn't there.

I recall the changes he went through. He was diagnosed with stomach ulcers at first and he was on a high, then he was told he had cancer and just six months to live, and he felt anger. He was in a terrific amount of pain and he didn't want it, didn't want it to go on. I feel anger that it went on for so long, to see a fit man suffer like that. In the last two months all he was doing was breathing, he wasted away to less than

The bridge over the river into Peterborough, with the Temperance Hotel and Midland Railway Warehouse to either side.

half his previous weight. I think one should consider euthanasia, until you've been through it yourself you can't understand. He understood there was no getting through it. Every day he was in more pain, feeling worse than the day before and to see a parent or loved one go through that is hard, you don't want to see that, and if there can be a mutual consent to save them that, there should be.

Paul Anger, born 1962

Loss of Sight

I still have a bit of sight, but was born with some sight loss, when I was at school they were convinced it was a behavioural problem. When I was little the doctor thought my behaviour was disruptive, for attention, because I didn't have a father. I remember going to Addenbrooke's Hospital and having lots and lots of tests. Before that, they thought I was playing a game, pretending I couldn't see the letters on the charts and going up to the blackboard to see things. They thought I wanted attention. The fact that I had to read things an inch away from my face seemed normal to me. At school people didn't want me on their team.

Lynne Hester, born 1960

Alcoholic

After my mother died we found bottles of whisky hidden all over the house. In the curtains, in the lounge, the wardrobe, and secret hidey-holes. You couldn't control what she was doing and, looking back, it was inevitable she would kill herself with it. She was unhappy at the idea of growing old. I only remember one incident when I was young, that she was drunk in the wrong context. She was drinking champagne in the middle of the day. She developed cirrhosis eventually. Her liver and kidneys ceased functioning and she died very quickly.

She collapsed at home, my father couldn't phone an ambulance because he can't speak. He managed to phone my brother and got him to understand something was wrong. An ambulance took her to hospital. My wife and I went there, it was January and the worst snow we'd had in ten years, it was a horrendous journey and took ten hours instead of four. The windscreen kept freezing up, that was three years ago, my mother was about sixty-eight. She was looking ahead to the way her mother had been; she had gangrene in her leg and had to have it amputated. My mother could see that happening to herself and didn't want it to happen. She drank more and more, as this played on her mind more and more, and nature took its course.

Steve Hill, born 1957

Son Keeps Me Going

A couple of times I've thought if it weren't for my son I'd have finished myself off a long time ago. I think if anything happened to me, what would happen to him? Sometimes he tells me, 'Love you mum'. He's polite with other people and says 'please and thank-you'. He's cheeky too, he has selective hearing when I tell him to do things.

Donna Mawby, born 1967

Bombing

I remember aeroplanes going over in the First World War. In one family they all died except this one boy.

Eleanor Bowers, born 1913

CHAPTER 9

Beliefs, fears and the future

A 1950s view of Ely Cathedral.

Iris Crossley on the beach, summer 1947.

Two Pews

Sundays were special days and we all went to church, the family took up two pews.

Iris Crossley, born 1924

Chapel

We lived at Shippea Hill on the Chivers Estate. Father was strict, and later became quite religious. Every Sunday we went to Sunday school, we would come home to dinner, then go to afternoon chapel. It was a Baptist chapel: Chivers were Baptist and nearly all the workers went to the chapel. The preachers were local but came from all over the area. One of them would always go on about the wickedness of the *News of the World* and Sunday opening shops in London. Another preacher would always hang his food bag on a hook near the pulpit. There was an old postman would do the Sunday p.m. services, they were quite interesting. My brothers and I would listen outside to find out what the hymn and text were, then we could tell father so he'd think we had attended. Meanwhile we were fooling around – jumping the dikes etc. Later father joined another chapel, Plymouth Brethren. The services were fire and brimstone, like the Salvation Army, if you wanted to go to Heaven you had to commit yourself to Christ. But the people were nice and friendly. In summer my brothers and I used to sit and read, things like *Treasure Island*. But my father disapproved, he wanted us to read religious books. I read *The Bible* right through, and *Pilgrim's Progress*.

Harry Bye, Born 1917

Head In The Clouds

I don't think much about religion. I'd like it if there were to be a God, but I'm not sure, I can't imagine a head in the clouds, watching over everybody! If someone asked me to describe God, I'd just say a head in the clouds. I don't pray and I wasn't christened either.

Frank Hamilton, born 1985

No Reason

I believe we must be here for some reason but I don't know why. Some people think there's a purpose but I can't see what, why are there living things? If you didn't have them you wouldn't need a world, but as we've got it, you might as well enjoy it, enjoy life. I don't always enjoy it, when there's so much stress on you, you've got deadlines to meet, but most of the time, life is there to be enjoyed.

Tim O'Connell, born 1984

Trinity

Once I was upset because a friend and I had grown apart and the support I received from God made me much stronger mentally, and able to withstand the trauma of losing this close friend.

When I speak about God, I speak about the Trinity. When I pray to the Lord, I pray to all three, the Lord is a Trinity. My parents take the view that my conversion is my choice, but I get on well with people who aren't Christian. Just because someone isn't a Christian doesn't mean that they're not a nice person. I feel okay they've made the choice, if they can stand by it and it's right for them, I have no problems with it.

Andrew Dunkley, born 1985

Heaven and Hell

The farmer who leased the land near us had the Wesleyan chapel built at the end of the field on the A1101, and there was a pub at the other end. So he said he would have Heaven at one end of his field and Hell at the other! They pulled Heaven down in the end – they

Haddenham High Street, 1930s.

Newtown, Huntingdon, 1900.

couldn't get a good congregation. But there was always a good congregation at the Pig and Whistle!

Harry Bye, Born 1917

Custodian

I feel an affinity for the land and am looking after it as a custodian and hoping to hand it on in good order. Its prime function is to produce food for the nation.

Anthony Pemberton, born 1942

Catholic

I was brought up as a Catholic and still believe in that, although my husband isn't Catholic. I believe in Heaven and Hell. I visualise Hell as being hot, flames and being burnt alive. Heaven will be nice, you'll be with your friends and family, an inner happiness, watching everything down below. Everyone needs something to believe in.

Louella Prince, born 1961

God Made The World

I know the people who come to church, but don't know that many people in the village. I like the church, because I've been brought up with religion, and I find it part of the weekly routine. I believe in God. He made the world, I believe he is always with me, I pray at home and in church. We pray for forgiveness, for food, to set right things that have gone wrong, and for people who aren't well. Also if you have something on your mind. I've had things on my mind, if I'm moving into a different class, I worry and get nervous. The worst thing that's happened to me has been growing up not knowing my father.

Syringa Fox, born 1989

Dance In The Aisles

I was brought up in the church, even though my parents stopped going when they were married. I was sent to church with my great-aunt Flo and cousin Janet. My own daughter used to dance in the aisles, one woman told me it was wonderful, that the spirit moved her. When I was young you weren't allowed to move a muscle!

Judy Fox, born 1955

Free

I have no great religious faith. I find it hard to believe in something I can't see, although I've felt there may be a bigger existence out there, I can't find the answer. We should value freedom, I feel freer than my parents, they didn't have the opportunity to go to university. For my generation, opportunities are there if you want to take them. Communities change so fast now.

Gavin Philpott, born 1980

Wary

The most important thing in life is to live free of fear and discrimination. I'm wary at work, how the customers might react, if they complained about my being gay, I might lose my job.

Edward Venni, born 1974

Not Religious

I'm not religious, my religion is that I've never done anyone a bad turn. I believe Christ walked this earth, was an influence, but not the Son of God or miracles. My parents were believers.

Jack Harrison, born 1907

Bleeding

As our communications get more and more clear and speedy, we need to think of our human relations as being much closer. Therefore, our problems are one another's: We cannot live tolerably in a situation in which we're okay, but other parts of the world are demonstrably bleeding to death. So it maybe that what we've done at the end of this century is to set up the challenges for the next.

Paul Crossley, born 1950

2000

The greatest resonance of the year 2000 is remembering how important it used to be when I was a child to think that the year 2000 would be the year I turned forty. That seemed much more significant then than it does now. I have lots of hopes as to my children, but nothing very specific. The

Paul Crossley in the Grantchester Tea Gardens, 1998.

twentieth century is full of great tragedy as well as great promises. The Holocaust and all the other genocides throughout the century sadly, thinking historically, are among the most outstanding things. But the conquering of them is also a huge lesson.

Molly Andrews, born 1959

Peace

I'd like to live to see my youngest daughter go to university and marry, and to see my older daughter marry, and to see my great-grandchildren. I hope there'll be peace, no more wars, and peace throughout the world. The twentieth century has been a good time for everybody, I have enjoyed my time so far, nearly half of it. We've learned so much, technology, medical advances, childbirth, people are living longer and that's definitely a good thing. The longer I live the better, so long as I don't get crotchety!

Sandra Wells, born 1955

No More Queues

The biggest change will be TV and computer shopping, no more long waits in Tescos or Sainsbury's, bread will arrive via robot controls. No more queuing, no more fiddling around waiting at the checkout, and that will be the biggest transformation of our lives, no going to the bank to get money, press a button and it'll come out. In 100 years time there'll be no more £1 notes or Euros, it'll all be done electronically, life will be easier but lazier, and people won't be doing things for themselves.

Peter Hoskison, born 1933

Looking Forward

When I was a little girl, I thought that if I reached the new millennium I would be sixty-five, and then I'd be happy to go! Now I'm looking forward to it.

Billie Bridgement, born 1935

Hard to Wrap Up

The twentieth century will be a hard one to wrap up, there are positive things we should be proud of. Most of us belong to the twentieth century, it's my century, but I look forward to the twenty-first century. It'll be interesting to see how it develops. I despair about the arguments over currency, it's how we get on together, as citizens of equal rights and to celebrate our differences. I would love to go to the march down the Garvahy Road in Northern Ireland, and enjoy it as a festival. I would love to stay in the twentieth century, but probably no one will let me!

Des Cusack, born 1942

Part Of Europe

When I retire I might do some supply teaching. I feel links with Europe are important so as not to be dominated by the USA. We need to be part of Europe, otherwise we'll be marginalised, sidelined, and not reap the benefits of the Euro. I like to wait and see before making a decision, the media do the opposite.

Richard Carter, born 1955

Optimistic

I'm optimistic about the future, but I worry, and feel lucky I haven't lived through any wars. I'm optimistic that this will continue, and that my son won't have to live through wars as well.

Lynne Hester, born 1960

Pessimistic

The shift to the new millennium is important. It's the great unknown, things happen so quickly and we can't go back, we've got to go forward. I'm mainly pessimistic about the future. If things were ideal, everybody would live together peacefully, and when there's a tragedy, that's when people help each other. It would be nice if that was the case all the time and caring about people, not being against others and blaming others for what happened.

Diana Philipott, born 1951

Nothing

The end of the twentieth century means nothing to me, the Millennium doesn't matter either, we have to put up with the future, what will be will be.

Louise Loveridge, born 1914

More Human

In the course of the twentieth century I've seen a slow but progressive movement towards the class system being less important. I consider it a great improvement. I have good relationships with waiters and porters in college – still no question as to who the boss is, but it's much more humane than it used to be. A classless society might be possible in another millennium, but that's the sort of thing that moves fairly slowly.

Prof. Brian Reddaway, born 1913

Celebrate

I think we're better off now, at the end of the twentieth century, than people used to be, because there are no classes, everyone's equal. Everyone can go to school and get a good education, and it's a much nicer atmosphere. The millennium changes matter, my dad has mixed views: 'I think it will be at the start of 2001'. I just ignore him and say, 'everyone else is celebrating the millennium, why can't we?' We're celebrating a thousand years gone by, a New Year, but it's special. The future will be more or less the same, we're still waiting for those hovering cars everyone has said for a long time we're going to get.

Frank Hamilton, born 1985

Anniversary celebrations of the birth of Oliver Cromwell, Huntingdon, April 1999.